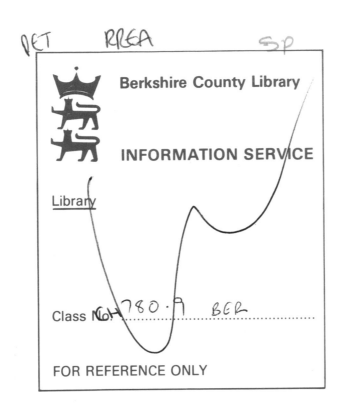

The Illustrated
History of Music

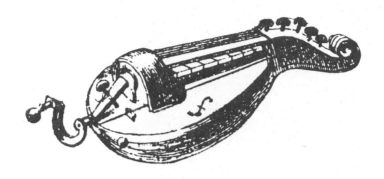

The Illustrated
History of
Music

By Vratislav Beránek

SUNBURST BOOKS

ACKNOWLEDGEMENTS

The publishers wish to thank the following institutions for their kind permission to reproduce photographs belonging to them or of their property:
Akademie věd České republiky, Prague
Hudební divadlo v Karlíně, Prague
Koninklijk Museum, Antwerp
Národní galerie, Prague
Petrof, Hradec Králové
Státní vědecká knihovna, Olomouc
Středočeská galerie, Prague
Supraphon, Prague

Text by Vratislav Beránek
Translated by Louise Doležalová
Illustrations by Milan Fibiger, Josef Jelínek, Zdenka Marschalová, Michal Skalník, Jindřich Ulrich
Photographs by Bohumil Beníček, Alexander Buchner, Jovan Dezort, Otto Dlabola, Jitka Dosoudilová, Jaroslav Hejzlar, Pavel Horník, Pavel Jasanský, Jan Králík, Štěpán Louda, Antonín Nový, Otakar Pernica, Ivan Prokop, Ivan Rájecký, Jaroslav Svoboda, Pavel Vácha
Graphic design by Václav Konečný
© A. C. L. Brussels (Hans Memling)

© Aventinum, Prague 1994

This edition published by Sunburst Books, Deacon House, 65 Old Church Street, London SW3 5BS, exclusively for Angus & Robertson of Australia.

ISBN 1 85778 025 6
Printed in the Slovak Republic
1/22/09/51-01

WEST GRID STAMP					
NN		RR		WW	
NT		RT		WO	
NC		RC		WL	
NH		RB		WM	
NL		RP		WT	
NV		RS		WA	
NM		RW		WR	
NB		RV		WS	
NE					
NP					

Frontispiece: *Music* by Josef Václav Myslbek (1848—1922).

Contents

Music is All Around Us

Music creates a background to our lives; it accompanies us from the cradle to the grave. It higlights our most important moments, rounds off both joyful and sad occasions, creates a good mood and provides food for thought. It is an invitation to dance, it can inspire pride in one's country and without it, neither ballet nor opera would exist. At a rock concert, it can lift the audience from their seats, and at a sports stadium it enlivens the atmosphere. It is heard in religious services; in the swelling organ at the height of celebration, and it is tranquillity in moments of meditation.

Music has many shapes; it is inseparable from our lives and our surroundings, but it has always had a serious competitor — the sounds of nature. The rustle of leaves, the songs of birds, the murmur of mountain streams, the roar of thunder and the chirruping of the crickets are all musical, but music itself is the creation of man, the product of his feelings and senses.

How is music shaped? What is it made of? Who creates it? When did it originate? Who invented it? Let us try to answer a few of these questions.

Anges musiciens **by Hans Memling, 15th century.**

A Message from the Past

Seeking the Beginning

There is no greater question we can ask than where did everything begin? We now know approximately how many millions of years have passed since the Earth took shape and how many more millions of years went by before *Homo sapiens* (thinking man) first evolved. On journeys into the past we discover step-by-step what early man looked like and how he lived. What we cannot know is what sounds he made or how he used his voice. We also do not know when a sound that we might call music first occurred. Even so, we cannot help asking how did music arise. Was it the result of human ingenuity, of chance, or did it evolve slowly through man's gradual refining of the sounds made by the creatures around him?

Ancient civilizations attributed a supernatural, magical meaning to music. They believed that music was a gift from heaven, from the gods, from fabulous messengers.

Can the pipe of a primeval hunter be considered a musical instrument? It probably had a quite practical purpose: to signal to other hunters and to summon assistance in capturing prey.

Left: A man wearing a goat skin is holding something that could be a musical instrument. Perhaps it has magical powers and can lure a herd of reindeer. Wall painting from the Les Trois Frères Cave in France, 15 000–10 000 BC.

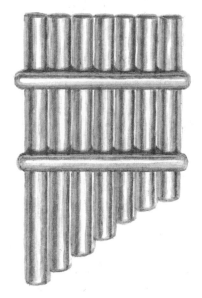

Above: The syrinx or panpipes. The tone is made by blowing across the straight-cut edge of the reeds.

Below: The ground bow, an instrument of African tribes. The string is fixed over a resonant piece of ground and stretched by a flexible bough. The sound is produced by plucking. The sound is mysterious, as if it comes from the ground.

For the Hindus, music was created by the god Brahma; the early Chinese learned scales from the legendary bird, the phoenix; the ancient Egyptians received music as a gift from Osiris, the god of the sun. The ancient Greeks believed that it was a gift from the god Apollo, and a famous Greek myth tells how Pan, the god of herds and forests, made the first musical instrument.

The Jews even had written 'proof' of the origin of music. In the book of Genesis, in the Old Testament, it states that Jubal, a descendant of Adam, 'was the father of all such as handle the harp and the organ'. There it was in black and white; and no one could deny Jubal his invention.

When looked at in the light of sober science, however, the problem of the origin of music has been tackled quite differently. Charles Darwin tried to clarify the matter when he claimed that primeval man made sounds for the same reason that birds sing in the mating season. Another theory suggests that ancient men communicated by using different levels of sound and that language developed from these. So, perhaps, speech grew out of a sort of early music. The theory closest to the truth, however, and one now supported by some scientists, is that music evolved from the primary cry of man, the sort of noise people make in anger or fear or to warn others of danger. From this, speech very gradually arose, and from excited speech a sort of musical expression or song developed.

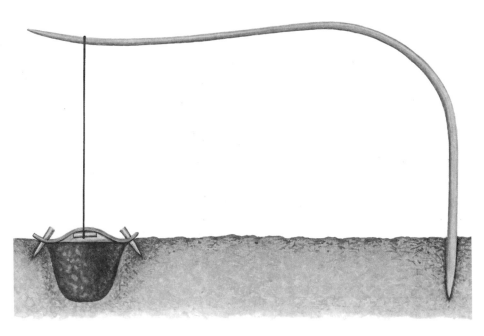

The slotted drum, one of many African drums.

Above: **The African drum on this picture is held under the arm. Altering the pressures on the cords changes the pitch of the stretched skin.**

Below: **A drummer from Guinea, in ceremonial attire, has an important role to play in magic rites.**

We know that early man liked to do things that were not necessarily useful or practical. For example, he would play with things he found around him. Perhaps in this way he discovered that certain objects make particular sounds: a hollow tree trunk produced a booming sound when struck, a whistle could be produced from a hollow bone, or a bowstring twanged when it was plucked.

From the very start, music had significance for man because he believed it had a hidden magic power that would help him to win the favour of the gods and ward off danger.

Early Man Talks to the 20th Century

We will never know the music of our Cro-Magnon forefathers (70 000–20 000 BC), but we can guess how it sounded and understand its importance by studying the culture of primitive tribes still living today, whose lifestyles are similar to those of Stone Age man. For these people, it seems that music is not something performed for others; nor is it simply a source of enjoyment and relaxation during leisure hours. Rather, it is a part of important rituals. Singing, rhythmic movements, the sound of instruments and dancing are combined to drive away evil spirits, avoid illness or to call up rain and a good harvest.

It is interesting that some African tribes do not communicate with words made up of vowels and consonants, but with groups of sounds delivered at varying pitch. A combination of high and low sounds produces a system of signals that have specific meanings. This is also true of the language of drums, also used by some African tribes. A message sent in what might be called 'drum language' can sometimes be heard over a distance of 20 kilometres (13 miles). It seems likely that our ancestors communicated using tones produced at different pitches. We can see how melody could develop from this, at first in a primitive form and then becoming increasingly complex.

Rhythm is the second main component of music. Rhythm is part of nature: day and night alternate, the seasons of the year follow each other with unchanging regularity. There is rhythm in walking, running and in the beating of our hearts. So the oldest percussion instruments were used primarily to produce rhythm, and the music of 'primitive' tribes is founded on the principle of rhythm.

Percussion instruments used by present-day 'primitive' tribes—the drum, for example—are similar to those used in primeval times. Africans hold drums in deep reverence. They serve many purposes: they can avert danger and heal the sick, accompany dancing and add to the sounds of battle. Drums are the instruments of ritual and are used to express reverence and to accompany sacrifice. Among some tribes, it is the custom to cut off a slaughtered enemy's finger and drop it through a special opening into a drum, to chase away evil spirits from the drum's sound. As the instruments of kings, drums were considered off-limits for ordinary people. In some tribes, the drum maker enjoyed special social status; indeed, a drum could be made only by someone who had received the king's personal favour.

With the gradual intermingling of melody and rhythm, music as we know it in modern western society came into being.

Discovering the Music of the Past

Although we have no proof of how music was performed thousands of years ago, as nothing that can be played or sung remains, archaeologists are uncovering evidence of the music of ancient civilizations. We can, therefore, guess at the sound of the musical instruments that exited. We can also learn the role music played in the everyday life of ancient peoples.

There are three kinds of evidence. Surviving musical instruments are, understandably, those that were made of materials which resisted the passage of time. The oldest of these are stone instruments, bone whistles; clay drums and, from more recent periods, wind instruments made of metal. The second, more widespread source of information comes from pictures of musicians in wall paintings, mosaics, vases and stone reliefs. Scientists can reproduce the instruments based on these pictures. This method of research is mainly used for ancient instruments, but we can also learn about the instruments of the Middle Ages from pictures. Written records from many different sources are the third sort of evidence. Some of these were made

Etruscans playing aulos and barbitons. Wall painting from 475 BC.

Egyptian musicians playing the Egyptian harp, the lute, the double oboe and the lyre. Tomb painting in Thebes-Veset, around 1420–1411 BC.

as systematic records, others were not. From these three sources we can begin to make a picture of what music consisted of in different times and in different parts of the world.

We know that in ancient Egypt, music belonged to the kings, queens and other important people. It also played a special role in Egyptian religious ceremonies. The Egyptians used instruments that still exist in somewhat different forms. Their stringed instruments included the harp and the lute, and their wind instruments were similar to the modern flute and oboe. They also used a variety of percussion instruments. Egyptian music had a formal structure that included both scales and intervals. This musical heritage eventually passed into the beginnings of European music.

In Asia, 3,000 years ago, the Chinese were able to calculate the sounds of all twelve tones and semi-tones of our scale. In practice, however, Chinese music was based on a five-tone, or pentatonic scale. This can be heard today in Oriental folk music. Spoken Chinese is a tone language and the meaning of words depends on their melodic sequence. This is why Chinese music developed from spoken sounds and musical instruments took second place.

There are many records of ancient Greek music. It was, for example, linked with drama, arts and the chorus was an essential part of an ancient Greek play. The Greek theory of music was formulated by the mathematician and philosopher Pythagoras (580–500 BC). His system of tone sequences or scales was later revised in the

Middle Ages and has continued into modern times. The scales of the medieval church were even given names adopted from Greek: Ionic, Doric, Frygic, Lydic, Mixolydic, Aeolic, although the scales were arranged differently from ancient

An Egyptian flute is depicted on the tomb of Pharoah Nencheftkal (5th dynasty).

Greek times. Greeks played string instruments, such as the harp, the lyre, and wind instruments. The aulos, for example, was something like an oboe. The strength of Greek influence on the development of European culture can be seen by the fact that the name for 'music' (in German *Music*, French *musique*, Italian *musica*, Russian *muzyka*) is derived from the Greek Muses, one of whom inspired music and all of whom were the companions of Apollo.

As in other arts, the Romans took over from the Greeks and developed the music they had inherited. The Romans knew how to work metal and could, therefore, make metal wind instruments. These were loud and their sound could be heard from far away across ranks of troops on the battlefield or resounding among the crowds during the triumphant parades of emperors. Roman horns included the straight metal tube, like a tuba; and the circular lituus, or bent horn, a cornu, which had a reed and a disc-shaped trumpet.

The Romans learned how to

Right: The lur, an ancient Roman bronze instrument.

Below: The olifant, a richly-carved ivory hunting horn. It is reminiscent of Roland, a famous paladin of Charlemagne, and the legend of his heroic death in battle against the Saracens in the Pyrenees in 778. The sound of this horn carried over immense distances and foretold the defeat of the besieged troops.

Greek instruments: the lyre, the aulos and the cithern (about 480 BC). Roman instruments: the cornu and the lituus (end of 4th century BC).

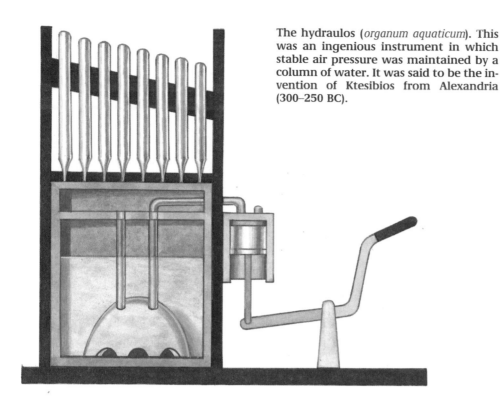

The hydraulos (*organum aquaticum*). This was an ingenious instrument in which stable air pressure was maintained by a column of water. It was said to be the invention of Ktesibios from Alexandria (300–250 BC).

make bronze instruments from the Etruscans, their rivals on the Apennine peninsula. We know this because a long metal tube, called the lur, found its way to the north of Europe. In the 19th century, lurs were found preserved in bogs along the Baltic coast and in Scandinavia.

Archaeological discoveries show that two lurs were always used together, their sounds carrying over the countryside in a harmonious duet.

A whistle-like instrument, the hydraulos, was perfected in Roman times. Remains of this predecessor of the organ were found in Pompeii. Air pumped by bellows sounded a system of pipes that were similar to panpipes. The air pressure was kept constant by a column of water, hence the instrument's name.

Fables and Legends

Order of the Gods

The ancient Greeks had a strong sense of order. This can be seen if you consider the hierarchy of their gods. The entire family of Greek gods lived on Mount Olympus, where the all-powerful Zeus ruled. He managed all the activities of the world and appointed members of his family to different responsibilities and ministerial posts.

The handsome Apollo ruled over the nine Muses. Each Muse was responsible for a particular art. Erato, for instance, had love poetry in her care. Euterpe was the goddess of lyric song, Calliope epic song, Clio was in charge of history, Melpomene cared for song and the theatre, especially tragedy, Thalia looked after comedy, Polhymnia was a minister of serious singing, Terpsichore watched over all dancing and Urania over astronomy.

In the lives of the Greek gods and goddesses, everything was in order and everyone who was active in science or the arts knew where he belonged and to whom he was responsible.

Legends about Apollo and the Muses are often revived in ballets and other performing and dramatic arts.

Adventures and Stories

Many of the gods and goddesses of ancient times were involved in singing, dancing and acting. For example Pan, who was in charge of the forests and the flocks, was once pursuing the nymph Syrinx with whom he had fallen in love. She fled from him into the river and changed into a reed before his eyes. Pan cut different lengths of the reed, arranged them according to size and fastened them together with wax, thus making the first musical instrument, the *syrinx*, or panpipes.

The Sound of Sirens

Although nowadays the sound of sirens usually means danger or something unpleasant, the Greek legends from which the word came concern dangerously charming creatures, half woman half bird, whose lovely songs carried across the sea. However, their beautiful songs were a trap, for the Sirens lured sailors to come to them and whoever succumbed forgot his home and slowly wasted away. Not even Homer's Odysseus was immune to their song as he travelled home from Troy. He was able to save himself and his crew only by stopping up his sailors' ears with wax and tying himself to the mast to avoid giving into temptation.

Above: **The Sirens—the temptation of Odysseus. Painting on a Greek vessel (*stamnos*), about 480–470 BC.**

Right: **Orpheus in a painting by a Baroque artist V. V. Reiner (1689–1743).**

Orpheus and Eurydice

The tale of Orpheus is a tragic one. Because he was so unhappy about the accidental death of his wife, Eurydice, he set out to find her in the Underworld. He must have been a splendid musician (he was said to have been taught by Apollo), for by singing and playing his lyre he was able to soften the hearts of the guardians of the deep and to go where no living mortal had ever been. The guardians surrendered Eurydice to him, but on one condition: Orpheus must not look at her, even once, until they returned home. Fearful lest she wasn't following him, he turned to look at his wife—and lost his beloved for ever.

David's Harp

Singers and musicians feature in the Old Testament. Music meant much to the Jewish people and a great deal has been passed down to us from Biblical times. Unfortunately, we do not know how the early Jews sang the Psalms; we have only the words. Nor do we know how King David played his harp. It became a symbol in his hands and was known as a 'royal' instrument.

Jericho

The story of how the trumpeters blew a powerful blast and the walls of Jericho came tumbling down is well known. While it is an

interesting story, physicists have raised serious objections. The trumpeters would have had to create a volume of noise many times in excess of that which can be tolerated by the human ear. In reality, no matter how hard they tried, the trumpeters would not have been able to knock down even a house of cards.

Looking Back to the Past

Even today, composers and choreographers constantly look back to the fables and legends of the past for inspiration. The stories and characters that fantasy has linked with music and singing are still used as subjects for contemporary works of art. For example, it is estimated that Orpheus and Eurydice feature in at least 70 operas, 12 operettas and 17 ballets. At the beginning of the 17th century, the story of Orpheus and Eurydice was a popular one and it was frequently set to music. Now a work of lasting importance, the opera *Orfeo* ('Orpheus'), by Christoph Willibald Gluck (1714–87), has been constantly performed for more than 200 years. The operetta by **Jacques Offenbach** (1819—80) *Orpheus in the Underworld* (1858) makes fun of the story and gives the legendary heroes the qualities of contemporary people. **Franz Liszt** (1811–86) honoured Orpheus as the symbol of the strength of the arts in a sound poem. **Igor Stravinsky** (1882–1971) also revived the legendary musician in his ballet *Orpheus*.

Apollo and the Muses occur in another of Stravinsky's ballets, called *Apollon Musagète*. Pan is the name given to a five-movement sound poem by the Czech composer **Vítězslav Novák** (1870–1949).

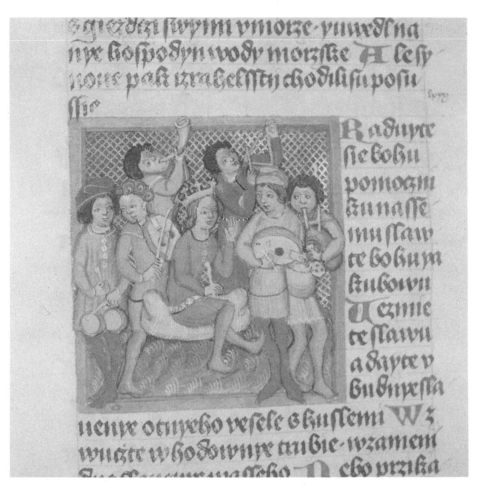

King David with musicians. An illustration from a medieval Bible (Olomouc, 1417).

Orpheus sings to the Thracians. Painting on a Greek vessel (*krater*), 460–440 BC.

Novák expressed his admiration for the gifts of nature, indicated by the names given to the separate movements of this extensive work: 'Prologue', 'Mountains', 'The Sea', 'Forests' and 'Woman'.

Claude Debussy (1862–1918) recalled the pipes of Pan in his small composition *Syrinx* for solo flute. Of greater importance and certainly very much better known, is his famous sound poem *Prélude à l'après-midi d'un faune*, dedicated to the little god who was changed from Pan to Faun in Roman religion. The Sirens, too, can be heard in the voices of the female choir in the third part of Debussy's *Nocturnes*.

The poetic heritage of the Old Testament was explored musically by **Antonín Dvořák** (1841–1904) in *Biblical Songs* and by Igor Stravinsky in *Symphony of Psalms*. The Psalms have inspired composers from the Renaissance to the present day, including Orlando di Lasso (1530–94), Johann Sebastian Bach (1685–1750), Johannes Brahms (1833–97), Franz Liszt and Anton Bruckner (1824–96).

King David, best known for his legendary struggle against the giant Goliath, is also a frequent source of inspiration for composers. Arthur Honegger (1892–1955) dedicated an oratorio to him and **Robert Schumann** (1810–56) chose him as a symbol for his life and work. Schumann, composer, virtuoso pianist, and writer, published a magazine called *Followers of David*. The subscribers to the magazine were supporters of everything progressive, waging battles over modern art in debates with traditionalists and conservatives. This clash between the old and the new was also the subject of Schumann's last piano composition in his cycle *The Carnival*, which he entitled 'March of David's Followers Against the Philistines'.

To the Honour and Praise of God

Pagans

Despite the incredible technical progress he has made, man is still helpless in the face of most natural catastrophes. Imagine, then, his helplessness in early times, when he was unable to explain much of what we take for granted. All power lay in the hands of supernatural beings, whatever name they were given. To keep on good terms with the gods, they had constantly to be wooed with sacrifices and devout prayers.

Our pagan ancestors accepted the importance of human sacrifice. Igor Stravinsky's ballet *Le Sacre du Printemps* ('The Rite of Spring', 1913) depicts pagan rites asking the earth to renew its natural forces in response to the sacrifical dance of a chosen maiden.

The invocation of spirits, accompanied by dancing and ecstatic cries and singing, is still a part of the rituals of many 'primitive' cultures. Even the early Christian church adopted a similar style and dancing, too, was included in early Christian ceremonies.

The Middle Ages, however, swept away all noise and ecstasy from religion, keeping only, as far as music was concerned, the sober singing of texts from the prayer book.

Right, above: **Invocation to the Sun, the eternal giver of life.**

Pagan rites were the theme of Igor Stravinsky's ballet *Le Sacre du Printemps.*

A Roman basilica. The Gregorian chant, a religious musical recitation in Latin, used to be sung here.

The Middle Ages

The best-known religious music of the Middle Ages is the Gregorian chant, so called because it is associated with Pope Gregory I (590–604). To modern ears the chanting may sound monotonous, the melody moving through only a few tones, the flow of the recitation only altering slightly to indicate the punctuation of the text.

In fact, the melodies were fixed by tradition and no one was permitted to make changes. At most, a chant could be ornamented slightly or be expanded with insertions. The chants were memorized and passed from generation to generation. For a long time it was not possible to write them down, as musical notation did not exist. At the end of the first century, tiny signs, known as neumes, appeared in the written texts. These indicated the approximate direction of the melody and acted as a support to the chanter's memory.

The Italian monk **Guido d'Arezzo** (*c.* 990–1050) introduced staves which made it possible to record the notes of the melody more accurately. Credit is also due to d'Arezzo for creating a system similar to our naming of notes as an

The beginning of the medieval system of musical notation. These strange signs (neumes) indicate the direction of the melody.

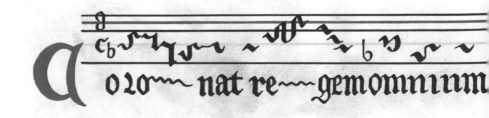

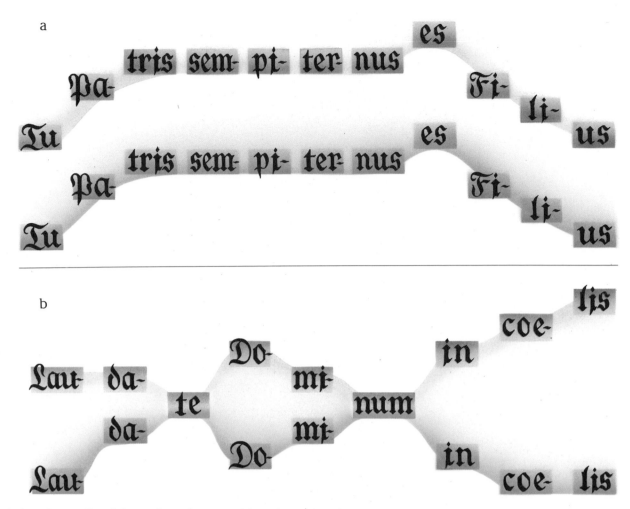

a

b

A diagram depicting the medieval duet. The voices sound in unison (a), or in counterpoint (b).

aid in remembering the relationship in pitch between tones. His system is based on the first syllable of the six verses of a Latin hymn in praise of St John: *Ut* queant laxis / *re*sonare fibris / *mi*ra gestorum / *fa*muli tuorum / *so*lve poluti / *la*bii reatum / sancte Johannes. D'Arezzo's creation is familiar in various forms. The sequence was completed by a seventh note *te*, and *ut* was replaced by the syllable *doh*, leaving: *doh, ray, me, fah, soh, lah, te, doh*.

The Christian Mass was filled with mystery. It was sung in Latin and the choir and the priest were separated from the congregation. In addition, the priest would turn his back to the congregation; in the Orthodox church today, the altar is still set apart by a screen.

At some point in the church service, two solo voices were sometimes heard. High and low voice sang together, combining two or more melodies. This is known as counterpoint. It has been preserved from medieval times to the present day.

This type of singing is known as polyphonic, meaning having many voices. It was cultivated in church music throughout Europe and was a product of the high point of the Middle Ages. Polyphonic compositions were gradually bound to a precise rhythm. This was regulated in advance and could not be changed at the whim of the composer. Only three variations, which corresponded symbolically with the Holy Trinity, were allowed. The first school of compos-

ers was centred around Notre Dame cathedral in Paris at the end of the 12th and beginning of the 13th centuries. The masters **Léonin** and **Pérotin** were associated with it.

Medieval music was founded on the melodic principle. Voices combined in a polyphonic composition without a thought for the consequences of harmony. The ability to understand and use harmony, rather than separate voices, did not develop until the Renaissance.

The Renaissance

The era of humanism, known today as the Renaissance, shone a new light on people's thinking and behaviour. Religious principles and the rigid rules of the

Music and singing have long been a part of funeral rites.

music was filling the then new, spacious cathedrals. This type of music had developed into a complex art, and one of its best composers was **Orlando di Lasso** (1532–94). Musical composition focused on the Mass. The unchanging part of the Mass, the 'Ordinary' (Kyrie, Gloria, Credo, Sanctus, Agnus Dei) was set to music many times. The base of the composition was the *cantus firmus*, or 'fixed song', which the other voices 'wrapped around' with their own melodies. Composers created complex works, but the voices were no longer entirely independent of each other, as in the music of the Middle Ages; the listener concentrated on the resulting harmony. Slowly, the organ and various other instruments found their way into the churches to accompany the singers. The music for the instruments did not differ to any great extent from that of the vocal parts—instruments and human voices interchangeable.

Composers of the time were seeking unusual sound effects. In St Mark's cathedral in Venice, for example, choirs were positioned on galleries opposite each other. They responded to each other in song, complementing each other in powerful harmony. This unusual and compelling style of composition for two choirs was the work of three composers and organ players at St Mark's: **Adrian Willaert** (*c.*1485–1562), **Andrea Gabrieli** (1510–86) and **Giovanni Gabrieli** (1557–1612). The stereophonic effect, which we take for granted today, was already understood and used during the Renaissance.

Music in England was also enjoying a golden age. Many types of folk songs were develop-

Church were shaken by the Reformation. The mystery surrounding religious rites was made clear and hymns were sung by everyone.

People sought greater pleasure in life. The aristocracy abandoned their castles; in France they built châteaux along the Loire, and Italian merchants constructed city palaces. Literature drew its inspiration from antiquity; drawing, painting and sculpture depicted things as they really were. Science was making new discoveries in astronomy, and seafarers were filling in the map of the world and creating naval powers. Johann Gutenberg's invention of book printing in 1445 opened up new era in European culture.

Richly developed polyphonic

ing and both popular and religious madrigals—songs for an unaccompanied group of singers—were becoming a feature of English music. Noteworthy composers of this period include **Thomas Morley** (1557–1603), **John Dowland** (1563–1626) and **William Byrd** (1543–1623). Byrd's compositions for the Anglican church equal any that were being produced on the Continent at that time.

With the Counter-Reformation, most European countries felt a renewed domination by the Church and a strengthened influence on cultural life. St Peter's basilica in Rome became an important centre for music. Its school of composers produced excellent church music, especially **Giovanni Pierluigi da Palestrina** (1525–94).

The musical works of the Renaissance period have not disappeared with time. Their indisputable excellence is still a source of pleasure, although today they are played more often in the concert hall than the church, often by consorts specializing in early music and instruments.

The Baroque Period

About 1600, a new epoch in European art was beginning. This new style, known as the Baroque, was first seen in architecture, when richly modelled shapes began to replace the restrained beauty of the Renaissance. Luxurious, aristocratic houses, with well-planned parks, were being built to demonstrate the power and wealth of royalty, the aristocracy and the church.

The dignified beauty of Baroque churches was impressive. Their dark corners were an invitation to meditation, while frescoes covering the illuminated vaults carried

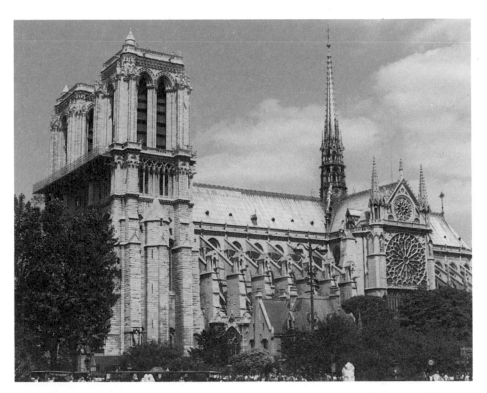

Notre Dame Cathedral in Paris was an important centre for music in the Middle Ages.

The start of the Reformation in Europe was linked, among other things, with the Bethlehem Chapel in Prague, where Master Jan Hus preached in the first decade of the 15th century and introduced into his services the idea of the whole congregation singing hymns.

eyes and thoughts upwards to the never-ending vastness of the heavens. Naves were filled with the powerful sound of the organ, other instruments and choristers. Candlelight and incense completed the evocative atmosphere.

A New Style—A New Content

Music, too, was changing its shape. Instruments were becoming independent of the voice. Techniques both for constructing and playing musical instruments were changing dramatically. The complex polyphony characteristic of the Middle Ages and Renaissance was replaced by simple melody with an accompaniment. At the same time, however, a new style of music was created that made use of the polyphonic art of the Renaissance: opera, a form of sung theatre, was taking shape. Soon its various components—arias, recitatives, choral passages—were adapted into a new form of church music, known as the oratorio.

In the oratorio, Biblical themes, evangelical texts and poetic compositions from the lives of the saints were created as large works for soloists, choirs, orchestra and organ. Passion plays, texts from Masses and stories from the Old Testament were all set to music. The church initiated the oratorio, but the style was determined by non-religious music that was mainly operatic. At first, oratorios were written in Latin, but soon they were being written in every European language—in German, Italian, French and English.

In Catholic countries, church musical festivals were supported by the aristocracy, while in Protestant Germany, their arrangement

St Mark's Cathedral in Venice and the Basilica of St Peter's in Rome, the largest church in the world, are associated with the best works of Renaissance composers.

was shared by the town burghers. Towns maintained church choirs and had special schools to train oratorio singers and instrumentalists. The St Thomas School in Leipzig, Germany, was one of the most famous.

At the beginning of the Baroque era in Germany, the best known composer was **Heinrich Schütz** (1585–1672), but the high-point of church composition was reached by **Johann Sebastian Bach**. Bach wrote about 200 church cantatas (solo pieces, sometimes with accompaniment) for St Thomas's.

These included the *Passion According to St John* and *St Matthew*. Bach used the melodies of the Protestant chorales in his organ preludes. Without doubt, his *Mass in B minor* is one of his most important works. His vast body of organ compositions, though really belonging to secular music, were played mainly in the churches—there were no organs anywhere else at that time.

Bach's contemporary **George Frideric Handel** (1685–1759) composed almost 30 oratorios that contributed greatly to the music of England, where he spent most of his life. He took his themes from the Bible, from ecclesiastical texts and from the myths and legends of antiquity. Some of his best known oratorios include *Messiah, Judas Maccabaeus, Semele* and *Solomon*.

Although most themes for oratorios came from religious texts, the form became a concert com-

The sound of the organ fills the glorious interior of the Baroque church.

Leipzig, where Johann Sebastian Bach composed his music. On the left the old school, on the right the Church of St Thomas.

Christ was dying, probably written by the Franciscan monk **Jacopone da Todi** (1230–1306), has been set to music many times by composers of all styles and periods, from Palestrina, through Haydn, Schubert, Liszt, Verdi, up to **Krzysztof Penderecki** (b.1933). The best-known setting of the **Stabat Mater** is Antonín Dvořák's. Here, he expresses all his sympathy with human suffering and his personal

Johann Sebastian Bach (1685–1750) and his three sons: Wilhelm Friedemann (1710–84), Carl Philipp Emanuel (1714–88), Johann Christian (1735–82).

George Frideric Handel

position that was frequently played outside the church, mainly in large theatres. Handel's oratorios, for example, were performed at the Covent Garden Theatre and the Royal Theatre, Haymarket, in London.

The Christian Tradition

Over a period of 2,000 years, Christianity became deeply rooted in the minds and actions of Western society and was a constant influence. We honour the humanistic ideals and moral commandments of Christianity, and our year is divided largely according to important dates in the Christian calendar. Even today, the arts often continue to serve the ideology of Christianity, but at the same

time draw inspiration from its heritage for the expression of thoughts that are far beyond its original religious intention. Modern works of art, even when based on the order of church ceremonies, also express ideas common to all people, regardless of religion.

A Mother was Standing

Stabat Mater dolorosa,
iuxta crucem lacrimosa,
dum pendebat Filius.

'The mother stood sorrowing,
beside the cross grieving,
on which her son was hanging.'

This medieval poem about the grief of the Virgin Mary as she stood beneath the cross on which

sorrow at the loss of his own children. When Dvořák's *Stabat Mater* was performed at London's Royal Albert Hall (1884), conducted by the composer himself, some 900 singers took part and the symphony orchestra consisted of 150 musicians.

Eternal Rest—the Requiem

*Requiem aeternam
dona eis, Domine . . .*

'Lord, grant them
eternal rest . . .'

Reflections on the meaning of life and on man's final hours resound constantly in works of art. A humble submission to fate, fear of the Last Judgement and a human desire for an existence beyond death—whether through belief in eternal life or in the remembrance of contemporaries—are concerns that have exercised many great artists. The text of the Latin Mass for the dead, the requiem, has, therefore, often provided the theme for important works of art. Like the oratorio, the requiem, too, outgrew the church service and became a concert piece in its own right. Let us look at the motives that gave rise to some works, and what was their fate.

Requiem, the last composition of **Wolfgang Amadeus Mozart** (1756–91), was written under mysterious and disturbing circumstances. The composer was visited by a secret messenger, who asked him to compose a requiem on behalf of an unknown benefactor. Although seriously ill, Mozart worked on the composition until death ended his untiring creative outpouring. The work was completed by his pupil **Franz Xaver Süssmayr** (1766–1803).

The Crucifixion was a frequent theme for works about human suffering. Mater Dolorosa under the Cross.

Et resurrexit tertia die—On the third day He arose from the dead . . . Alleluia. Let us rejoice . . .

Sixty-year-old **Giuseppe Verdi** (1813–1901) dedicated his mighty *Requiem* to the memory of the poet Alessandro Manzoni, an important figure in the struggle for the unification of Italy. It was composed for an unusually large group of performers—soloists, a choir and an orchestra. Apart from his operas, this is Verdi's largest work.

For sheer grandness, Verdi's *Requiem* is surpassed only by the immense *Grande messe des morts* (Requiem Mass) by **Hector Berlioz** (1803–69). Apart from the choir and a large symphony orchestra, this calls for four brass bands to play from different positions in the concert hall. From the four points of the compass, trumpets, trombones and tubas summon the dead to the Last Judgement, timpani storm the wail of lost souls and the prayers of the blessed can be heard. Berlioz, who was only 33 years old when he composed the work, demonstrated a supreme mastery of orchestral sound and created a thrilling and dramatic masterpiece. The *Grande messe des morts* had its première in 1837 at the Dôme des Invalides in Paris, the only concert hall where it could be performed to its best advantage and for which Berlioz had composed it.

Antonín Dvořák's *Requiem Mass* poured forth from the composer's sincere religious devotion as an intimate confession, a coming to terms with the inevitability of fate, even though he wrote the score at a time of full creative vigour and buoyant vitality.

Among these great works, we must also include the *War Requiem* for solo, mixed choir and orchestra by **Benjamin Britten** (1913–76). This was first performed in 1962 to mark the restoration of Coventry Cathedral, which had been destroyed when the city was bombed in 1940. The

Leoš Janáček

composition was dedicated to the memory of Britten's friends who fell in World War II.

Glory to God in the Highest

Gloria in excelsis Deo . . .

The most frequently performed sacred work is the Latin Mass. The Mass reached its peak during the Renaissance, with the work of Palestrina, and it weaves continuously to the present day. Like the requiem, its theme is interpreted in a variety of ways from the profound devotion of Bach's *Mass in B minor*, to present-day works in which composers present new, topical meanings.

With his grand *Missa solemnis* (1823), **Ludwig van Beethoven** (1770–1827) produced a composition that cannot even be performed during a church service without it being cut short. It is like a concert oratorio, in which the composer expresses his relationship with God, man and nature. The *Missa solemnis* was composed during the same period as the *Ninth Symphony* and forms its counterpart.

Dôme des Invalides, Paris, the place where the first performance of Berlioz's *Requiem Mass* was given.

JANÁČEK MŠA GLAGOLSKAJA
GLAGOLITIC MASS

Söderström / Drobková / Livora / Novák / Hora (organ)
Czech Philharmonic Chorus and Orchestra
Sir Charles Mackerras

The *Glagolitic Mass,* the never-aging music of the ever 'young' composer, Leoš Janáček.

The profoundly devout Franz Liszt composed a solemn Mass for the consecration of a cathedral in Hungary.

A far less traditional composition is **Bohuslav Martinů's** (1890–1959) *Drumhead Mass*, written at the beginning of World War II. Liturgical texts blend with excerpts from the Psalms and contemporary verse. The Mass expressed the feelings of a soldier longing for home, his anxiety and defiance, his prayers and his hopes. It is unusually scored, written for male voices and mostly wind and percussion instruments because it was originally intended to be performed in the open air.

The *Glagolitic Mass* (1926) by **Leoš Janáček** (1854–1928) is really unique. Although it is based on the customary order of the Mass, it takes a completely non-traditional approach. The words of the Mass are in Old Church Slavonic, a language used in the churches of the composer's native land before the introduction of the Latin liturgy. It is not an appeal to God in the religious sense. The music is primarily temperamental and exultant, a celebration of man and nature, a proclamation of faith in life. Janáček wrote it when he was 72 years old.

Music for Pleasure

The story told in the preceding pages has carried us from fervent prayers and choir singing through to music that is more secular than religious. Calling this chapter Music for Pleasure might mean that we are leaving holy places, coming out of the churches and throwing ourselves into a whirlpool of enjoyment at fairs and in taverns, out of sight of strict church moralists. By no means! Let us stay for a moment under the vault of a Gothic cathedral, which, in the

Above: **A troubadour, a medieval singer of love songs, pictured by an artist of a later date.**

Left: **Jan Steen (1626–79),** *Serenade.* **A cheerful group of people play a noisy serenade, probably at a carnival.**

remote Middle Ages, was more than once witness to high-spirited festivities, where not only laymen but also those from the clergy made merry.

New Year is a relic of the so-called Saturnalia, a pagan celebration in honour of Saturn, the god of agriculture. With the silent consent of the church, much revelry took place, including the Festival of Fools, during which people danced in churches, shouted and drank and did unheard of things. And what about the processions through the streets? Even today there would be objections to the content of the songs and the pantomimes that were so enthusiastically applauded by the onlookers. Similarly, the Festival of the Ass, which was intended to recall the flight of the Holy Family into Egypt, had a decidedly secular, even vulgar, atmosphere. A live donkey would be led before the church altar where people would sing in unison 'hee-haw', and a hymn would resound throughout the church to the honour of His Royal Highness the Ass!

Parlez-moi d'Amour

Now we shall sing of love, for Cupid's arrows have struck singers from time immemorial. When the Crusades ended, the knights could shed their armour and walk with a lighter step; it was time to devote oneself to pleasant things. So knights became poets, singing the praises of love and conquering the hearts of noble ladies.

The *troubadours* of Provence in southern France and the *trouvères* of northern France were always welcome guests in the castle halls. They were accompanied by jugglers and minstrels, who enhanced their songs with instrumental accompaniments. Jugglers also performed in market squares and amused the public with their stunts, which were more comical than musical.

Apart from lyrical subjects, such as love, loyalty, friendship and bravery, the songs of the *troubadours* and *trouvères* also told epic tales, calling to mind the heroic deeds of both recent and more distant times. Some of the best-known French love songsters include Bernard de Ventadorn, Guillaume de Poitiers, Duke of Aquitaine, Chrétien de Troyes, Thibaud de Champagne and, especially, the famous Adam de la Halle.

The poetry of chivalry spread from France to Germany, where the minstrels were called *Minnesängers* (*Minne* = love). The best of these were Walther von der Vogelweide, Wolfram von Eschenbach and Heinrich von Meissen, known as Frauenlob.

Neither Giuseppe Verdi's opera *Il Trovatore* ('The Troubadour') nor **Richard Wagner**'s *Tannhäuser* is the musical dramatization of a historic event, but rather a romantic 19th-century nostalgia for the Middle Ages. The libretto, or story, of Wagner's opera leads up to a singer's tournament at Wartburg Castle and contrasts the op-

Above: **A medieval illustration to verses that were later set to music by Carl Orff.**

Right: **In Richard Wagner's opera *Tannhäuser*, the knights fight at Wartburg Castle.**

posing attractions of passion and pure love. In Verdi's opera, the conflicting emotions of love, vengeance, self-sacrifice and jealousy are stirred up to the highest point. The conflicts are solved through the death of the hero. The troubadour Manrico and the knight Tannhäuser have the opportunity on stage to reach the apex of singing, although in a very different form from that of their predecessors.

At the Royal Court

During the Middle Ages music was part of court life. The art of the *troubadours* and the *trouvères* was replaced progressively by more complex polyphonic music, and court society was entertained with song. The canon, a round song in which individual voices begin to sing the same melody one after the other, became popular. A rare relic of the 13th century is a six-voice English summer canon, 'Summer is icumen in'.

In the next century, the composer **Guillaume de Machaut** (1300–77) was engaged at the French court. He created a new type of secular, polyphonic composition in which the top sung melody was accompanied by one or more instruments.

With a Glass of Wine

During the Middle Ages, merry groups of students and mischievous schoolboys would wander from town to town and from university to university. They were called *vaganti*, or vagrants. They were educated, had a broad outlook on life and were able to enjoy themselves. They found no difficulty, for example, in composing verses that ingeniously alternated Latin and other languages. They made fun of disorder, sang about love and made rhymes about quite ordinary things. They even made fun of serious liturgical texts, such as

Dies irae, dies illa
solvet saeclum in favilla.

This opening couplet of a sequence about the Last Judgement, a part of the Requiem Mass, was changed by the students to:

Bibit ille, bibit illa,
bibit servus cum ancilla . . .

'He drinks, so does she,
the serving maid and the
lackey . . .'

The verses come from a volume dating from the end of the 13th century, which was discovered in a Benedictine monastery in Bavaria. The words were put to music by **Carl Orff** (1895–1982) in a cantata for solo, choir and

Hommage à Machaut

Ars cameralis

Right, above: Hommage à Machaut **is a tribute to the composer Guillaume de Machaut. This music from the 14th century has been revived on a current LP.**

Many student songs of the Middle Ages were born over a glass of wine.

orchestra, *Carmina Burana* (1936). The songs are about happiness, spring, the kingdom of love and, of course, about creating a good mood while imbibing a good beverage.

Laurels for the Mastersingers

Today we are quite used to singers gathering together at festivals and competing for the best popular song, to record companies producing records, tapes and CDs, which are assessed according to the number sold, and to the huge wheel of big business that turns constantly around popular performers. But how were the singers and musicians of the ages past rewarded?

The Minnesängers used to sing the praises of chivalry, love and loyalty in castle halls, trying to win the hearts of their chosen ladies. Their heritage passed from castles to towns and developed into the art of the Mastersinger, or Meistersinger. Knights gave way to burghers. Cobblers, bakers, goldsmiths, leather-workers, boiler-makers, metalworkers, tinsmiths, and soapmakers were all associated in guilds of singers. They composed poems and music and they had their apprentices and journeymen. Their music production was governed by strict rules and they performed their works at song festivals. Many German cities, such as Mainz, Frankfurt-am-Main, Strassburg and Munich, had associations of Mastersingers. The best known of them all, thanks to Richard Wagner, was Nuremberg.

In his opera *Die Meistersinger von Nürnberg* ('The Mastersingers of Nuremberg', 1867), which is the comic opposite of his *Tannhäuser*, Wagner depicted townspeople in the mid-16th century and their

A statue of Hans Sachs in Nuremberg. The master has just changed his shoemaker's hammer for the pen of a poet.

honest artistic endeavours. In doing so, he settled accounts with the cities that rejected his modern artistic style. In the character of the writer Sixtus Beckmesser—originally he was to have been named Hans Lick—who knows all the rules but little else, Wagner made fun of his opponents, especially the main representative of his conservative critics, Eduard Hanslick.

The opera culminates in a meet-ing of the singers. The winner hands his prize—a symbolic laurel wreath—to the one who is thought to be first among the Mastersingers. His name has gone down in history: the shoemaker poet, and Mastersinger, Hans Sachs.

Music Comes Home

The time came when music no longer needed to depend upon

service to the church. Apart from elevating minds to religious heights, music is also capable of providing man with quite simple everyday pleasure, of entertaining him with an interplay of tones and wit. During the Renaissance, the road taken by music divided in two; the two paths did not turn their backs on one another, but continued in parallel. One influenced the other; they borrowed technical skills from each other and at times, would accept finished works from each other, but furnished with different texts.

The motet, a polyphonic church composition from the 16th century, has its counterpart in the secular madrigal. The music is the same, only the words are different. The singing of madrigals used to entertain both the aristocracy and the middle classes in Italy, while in France its counterpart was the *chanson*.

The madrigal contributed to the birth of opera at the end of the 16th and beginning of the 17th centuries. At that time, comedies were being performed in Italian theatres in which the dialogue, which should ideally have been sung by solo voices, was instead sung by a polyphonic choir accompanying the pantomime performance of the actors.

Instruments, such as the lute and the virginal, began to appear in homes and compositions were being written for amateur music-making. Music had not yet reached the level of what is now

Left: **The closing scene from Richard Wagner's opera** *Die Meistersinger von Nürnberg.*

The ballads of marketplace singers were printed on broadsheets. This song tells of 'the most strange comet which has been spotted on the Turkish border'.

Travelling players stage a show from their repertoire.

called a concert; people sang and played for their own enjoyment. Later, when the aristocracy put together their own orchestras, the audience would sit on one side and the performers on the other. Should the master of the house invite his friends in order to show off his musicians, then he would 'give a concert'. The phrase 'to give a concert' has survived in German, French and English to this day.

Under the Blue Sky

Today, only circuses and a few other performing companies travel from town to town. These people are the descendants of the travelling players, jugglers, magicians and acrobats who used to travel the dusty roads in canvas-topped carts, stopping to erect their simple stages on village greens, in market-places or in areas set aside outside towns. These people were not members of respectable society and townspeople behaved towards

them with some reserve. Their performances often included singing. They sang about things that were happening in the world, what people were complaining about, what was worrying them or what they desired. They presented topical news in song in an entertaining way. The songs, printed on small leaflets, were sold on the spot.

Let us travel to Paris. It is the mid-17th century, the time when Molière's comedies were being played to high society at the Palais Royal or at Versailles and when all kinds of entertainment could be found on the bridges of Paris, especially the Pont Neuf. People flocked to hear their favourite singers and their songs. New, topical texts were written using well-known melodies so that the audience could easily join in with the performers. This later gave rise to a form of folk theatre, vaudeville. Later vaudeville developed into comic opera. From the bridges of Paris, the road for French singers and their *chansons* leads to the cabarets in Montmartre and to the music halls and the stage of Olympia.

Vienna is Set Whirling

The waltz developed out of a dance that originated somewhere in the Austrian Alps. The dance was called the Ländler. It had a simple melody to which people danced, sang or yodelled. It was brought to Vienna by village players, who went round the taverns in the suburbs making music for dances.

It acquired an urban style in its music and dance movements and was also given a new name—the waltz. The German verb *walzen*, meaning to revolve, expresses its

37

Even today on the streets of Paris, you may meet roaming musicians whose instruments are operated by turning a handle.

hesitate to recall this fact in the finale of his opera, and he mixed the popular waltz melody into the production as if his musicians were playing at a banquet.

The airy, carefree, graceful movement and the charm of the waltz melody fully expressed the mood of the city on the Danube. It was in the winter of 1814–15, at the time of the Vienna Congress, when a new arrangement of Europe was being discussed following the Napoleonic wars, that the waltz got into full swing. Vienna was full of important guests for whom splendid entertainment was arranged every day. The entire city was taken over by the three-beat dance.

character. The quicker tempo of the waltz and the smooth, supple, rotating dance movements were fun. The waltz remained on the outskirts of town (and society) for quite some time. In high-society *salons*, ladies in crinolines and gentlemen in powdered wigs perfected the strict order of the minuet, the gavotte and the quadrille.

Moralists protested against the waltz's relaxed character and the holding of partners. Dance masters also objected; in contrast with the more usual complicated dancing line, the waltz was so simple they had nothing to teach!

At first the dance did not even have a name; it was simply called *Deutscher Tanz*, 'the German dance'. For a long time both names were used. German dances, that is waltzes, were even composed by first-rank composers, such as Mozart, Beethoven and Schubert.

Suddenly, the waltz appeared on stage in an unimportant opera and at once it became the fashion for the Viennese. The opera was called *Una cosa rara* and its composer was the now long-forgotten Vincenzo Martini. The year was 1787, the same year that Mozart wrote *Don Giovanni.* With a measure of irony, Mozart did not

First Vienna, Next the World

Important composers of the waltz soon came forward, especially **Joseph Lanner** (1801–43) and **Johann Strauss** (1804–49), who

You may see a large part of Paris from the Arc de Triomphe (1) and all of it from the Eiffel Tower (4). The plan shows well-known places linked with both serious and light music, from the past and the present: Opera (2), Moulin Rouge (3), Palais du Louvre (5), Palais Royal (6), Pont Neuf (7), Odéon (8), Notre Dame (9).

New ballroom dances were invented at the end of the 18th century, the most popular of them being the waltz.

with their orchestras spread the new music far beyond the borders of the Austrian Empire. Then **Johann Strauss the Younger** (1825–99) became the star of dance and concert halls and was eagerly sought throughout Europe and overseas. In Boston, Massachusetts, some 30,000 people attended a concert of Strauss's orchestra, and 800 musicians performed his waltz *The Blue Danube*. They had to be guided by 100 assistant conductors. That waltz became the musical symbol of Vienna and has remained so to this day.

The quality of the waltzes composed by Josef Lanner and the two Strausses—their pleasant melodies which caught the mood of the Viennese world—influenced the creation of new dances around the world and affected the composition of serious music. Idealized waltzes or echoes of waltz melodies were written by Frédéric Chopin, Robert Schumann, and Franz Liszt. The waltz became a part of operatic, balletic and symphonic productions. It is heard in the second movement of Berlioz's *Symphonie Fantastique* in the ballroom scene. We find it in the world of Carl Maria von Weber (1786–1826) and in the ballets and symphonies of Pyotr Ilyich Tchaikovsky (1840–93). It is a basic component of Richard Strauss's (1864–1949) opera *Der Rosenkavalier*. But above all, the waltz is the musical cornerstone of the Viennese operettas of Strauss and Lehár, which are discussed in a

Johann Strauss the Younger, the immortal composer of waltzes and operettas, has won the gratitude of the Viennese.

Left: **Johann Strauss's most popular waltz,** *The Blue Danube,* **is played in a great variety of arrangements. This one is for a male voice choir and orchestra.**

later chapter. If someone compiled a list of the age of dances, then the waltz would certainly take first place. It has already lived for more than 200 years.

The World Dances the Polka

In the 1830s, a new social dance appeared in Bohemia. No one is sure where it came from. It is a fact, however, that the brisk rhythm of the polka—its simple melody and understandable form—fitted the feelings of the young people of that time. Suddenly, the polka's popularity spread across Europe with the speed of an explosion, just as the waltz had. The composers of polkas did not achieve the musical standard of the waltzes of Johann Strauss, but even so the polka reigned in the dance halls of the world.

Left: **The polka, a dance of lively optimism. Here, it is performed in** *The Bartered Bride,* **an opera by Bedřich Smetana.**

Jazz is Born

It was the end of the American Civil War—the war between the states. In New Orleans, the largest port in the southern United States, lived a multi-racial society made up of whites, blacks and people of mixed parentage. Black people, released from slavery, were now able to earn their living as hired workmen. Some of them made their mark as excellent musicians, perhaps because they had

The main street of New Orleans, Canal Street, at the beginning of the present century.

Members of the Count Basie Band.

Louis Armstrong, a great figure in jazz history.

retained something from the home of their ancestors in Africa: a unique musicality and especially a sense for thrilling arrangements and the ability to improvise. These people obtained instruments from former military brass bands and without being able to read music, learned to play them. They played in open spaces and in places of entertainment and were successful mainly because the spontaneity of their playing was more exciting than the staid playing of white musicians. Black marching bands were the centrepoint of a new type of music that later, when joined by white and other musical influences grew into jazz.

Let us take a brief look at one or two stages in its history.

Ragtime

While ragtime was not yet jazz, it represented the first attempts to combine black rhythm with European music. An original way of playing the piano appeared when, over the rhythmically steady accompaniment of the left hand,

Left: **New Orleans' harbour. Music that spread to all parts of the world was played on these paddle steamers.**

42

the right hand performed a syncopated melody (accenting the beat that usually is not accented). This style of playing the piano was soon taken over by other instruments. Ragtime made its appearance at the World Fair in Chicago in 1893. **Scott Joplin** (1868–1917), became the classic composer of ragtime. His best-known composition, *The Entertainer*, found its place among the collection of evergreens.

The gramophone record stirred up interest in new kinds of popular music.

COLUMBIA

At the beginning of the 20th century and later, ragtime penetrated into the compositions of several prominent composers, such as Claude Debussy, Igor Stravinsky, and Paul Hindemith.

'Ol' Man River'

While huge paddle steamers travelled up and down the Mississippi River, on board bands were playing to entertain the passengers. In this way, the musicians of the Deep South reached the large cities of more northern states— Memphis, St Louis and then on to Chicago. Some of them stayed

there and did not return. Others carried the new music into the cultural and commercial centre of the United States—to New York City.

The Land of Ten Dollars

Before the new wave of music had even crossed the ocean, Dixieland was born. Where did its name come from? Maybe it was taken from the name of one of two surveyors, Mason and Dixon, who determined the line that separated the South from the rest of the United states. Dixie was also the name given to the ten-dollar banknote issued in New Orleans

Seven Jazz Comedians touring Europe—an advertisement dating from 1933.

before the Civil War. The French numeral *dix* (ten) was printed on the note, and it was called a 'dixie'.

The name chosen by a group of five white musicians—the Original Dixieland Jazz Band—indicates where the music came from. Their instruments were cornet, clarinet, trombone, piano and drums. Before the end of World War I, they had started to make records.

Jazz Captivates the Continent

World War I was over. Once again the time was right for cheerful music to flourish; people wanted to enjoy themselves and make the best of life. Records and the first jazz bands were bringing a new, dynamic sound that was irresistible to Europe. Under the term 'jazz' came a flood of new dances, including some from South America, which had nothing more in common with jazz than the instruments being played. Every band that included a saxophone, brass instruments, piano and drums was called a jazz band. Boisterous young people, as well as respectable ladies and gentlemen, caught jazz fever and learned the new dances. The record industry produced millions of black discs and flooded the world with music that was radically different from anything it had ever heard before. A new era, in which new styles and methods of composition, instruments, arrangements and instrumental interpretation become quickly popular and faded just as fast, had begun.

George Gershwin's music stands on the bordeline between two worlds: jazz and symphonic music. This is a recording of the symphonic poem *An American in Paris* and *Rhapsody in Blue*.

Left: **No jazz band was complete without a saxophone.**

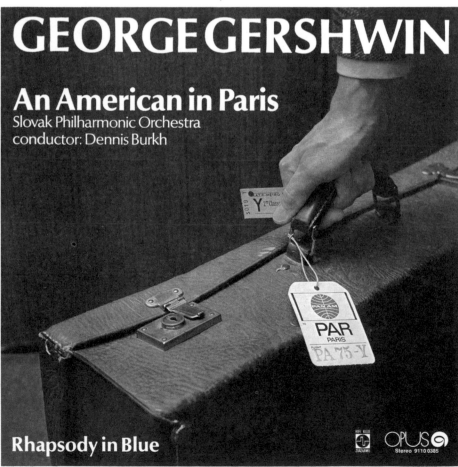

GEORGE GERSHWIN

An American in Paris
Slovak Philharmonic Orchestra
conductor: Dennis Burkh

Rhapsody in Blue

OPUS
Stereo 9110 0385

Lionel Hampton, an American vibraphonist.

A swing band with a large number of musicians.

Inspiration

Out of a general enthusiasm for jazz, claims were made that here lay the regeneration of music and that only jazz is the music of the future. Indeed, jazz provided interesting inspiration for a number of composers. Its rhythms stirred the music of Igor Stravinsky, Paul Hindemith (1895–1963), Darius Milhaud (1892–1974), Ernst Křenek (1900–91) and also Bohuslav Martinů. After a time, however, the fragrance of the new spice faded. Classical music returned to the means of expression peculiar to it and through which it is able to develop musical ideas into broad areas and serious artistic communication.

Even so, jazz found a composer who attempted an expansive music form filled with jazz, a so-called 'symphonic jazz', with some success. His name was **George Gershwin** (1898–1937). His piano concerto, his two rhapsodies, especially *Rhapsody in Blue*, his symphonic poem *An American in Paris* and his jazz opera *Porgy and Bess* are compositions that still attract us by their melodic invention, their ravishing rhythms and their instrumental colour.

Pages from History

Today, jazz is as much at home in Europe as it is in the United States. It has developed rapidly, as can be seen in the following survey of its stages and styles.

Swing

In the mid-1930s, when the world was recovering from economic crisis and war was not yet a threat, the traditionally small jazz bands reshaped themselves into big

Stephane Grappelli, the famous jazz violinist.

bands that filled dance halls with the compact sound of saxophones, trumpets and trombones, supported by the rhythm section made up of piano, percussion instruments and double bass.

The differences between 'true' jazz, with its essential improvisation and popular dance music, were gradually swept away. There was extraordinary development in the skill of instrumentalists, and composers and arrangers could count on perfect interpretation. History records a number of important and influential names from the swing era, such as **Benny Goodman** (1909–86), **Woody Herman** (1913–87) and **Glenn Miller** (1904–44).

Bop

In the 1940s, black musicians were once again leading the development in jazz. In opposition to the order and restrained delivery of swing bands, improvisation once more came to the fore, often with completely uninhibited performances breaking all previous rules and full of bright ideas and brilliant musicality. The path led from there to modern jazz. Let us recall a few legendary names of this epoch, such as trumpet player **Dizzy Gillespie** (b. 1917), alto saxophone player **Charlie 'Bird' Parker** (1920–55) and pianist **Arthur (Art) Tatum** (1909–56).

Cool

Yet again, there was a reaction to the developments of the immediate past. After the virtuosity and complexity of bop came a balanced, moderate music with a new timbre, using a combination of instruments so far unusual in jazz. This new direction attempted to combine jazz with classical music, and it later emerged as music of the so-called 'third stream'. Because the new style of playing was predominant in orchestras from the West Coast of the United States, California in particular, it got the name of West Coast jazz.

Hard Bop

Once more, black musicians came to the fore, linking the 1950s and 1960s with the style that had resulted in bop and stressing the original traditions of black culture. As they were mainly performing in New York City, the style was described as East Coast jazz.

Free Jazz

Over the centuries, European music had created a collection of laws and rules. The new wave of jazz in the late 1950s and 1960s, mainly driven by black musicians, pushed aside the obligation to be guided by rules. Unusual sounds were coaxed from instruments; it was in the sphere of classical music and at the time of the sound experiments called New Music.

Jazz Rock and Rock 'n' Roll

From the 1960s, a simpler type of Afro-American music moved into the music scene: rock, with fully electrified instruments, synthesizers, microphones and loud-speakers, and with engineers whose equipment was capable of turning a simple musical expression into a noise bordering on the limits of perception. Rock also influenced jazz, which took from it electrical instruments and the simpler rhythmic aspects. On the other

From the star-strewn sky of popular music:

Dizzy Gillespie, a fixed star or a comet?

Elvis Presley *(above)*

B. B. King *(above)*   Noel Neal *(below)*

Chick Corea *(above)*   Ray Charles *(below)*

The Beatles—John Lennon, Paul McCartney, George Harrison and Ringo Starr—on the steps of the plane that was to take them on their famous tour of the United States in 1966.

work because, like the forerunners of jazz 100 years ago, the first pioneers of rock came from the American South. Chief among them, though, was the white singer **Elvis Presley** (1935–77).

The rock era called into being groups whose members composed and interpreted their own songs. An explosion of pop music was in the making. The first act took place in England.

The Silver Beatles

First called The Silver Beatles, they later shortened the name of their group simply to The Beatles. The essence of their music and their performances was a strongly expressed, rhythmic pulse—the Mersey beat.

They were barely 15 years old, when the four boys from Liverpool got together. They had a lot to learn. They started as amateurs, hardly able to read music, but within a few years, they were the most famous pop group in the world. The Beatles suited their contemporaries exactly. Their appearance and behaviour were exciting and the content of their songs expressed the feelings of their generation. The Beatles established a dialogue between performers and audience. Their music created a large number of imitators and aroused an interest in active amateur music-making. They unleashed an electric storm of sound of unheard of intensity. Meanwhile, one of their best-known songs, *Yesterday*, was accompanied by a string quartet.

The huge popularity of The Beatles has not been equalled by any of the groups who followed. The Eagles, for example, who were in a way the heirs to The

hand, rock musicians learned quite a few things from their musically more mature jazz colleagues. An outstanding personality in this period was the pianist **Chick Corea** (b. 1941).

Rock, which is a shortened ver-sion of the original Rock 'n' Roll, has permanently influenced all pop music. Its singers use strong forms of expression, full of personal involvement, in a way that is characteristic of black musicians. Here too, black influence is at

Mick Jagger, one of the members of the popular group, The Rolling Stones.

The Rolling Stones, who followed The Beatles to fame. From the left: Ron Wood, Mick Jagger, Keith Richard.

Beatles, were from the West Coast and produced pleasantly harmonized songs; but they never possessed the same 'magic'.

The Star-strewn Skies

Star billing on concert programmes of classical music is always given to the composer and his work, and the interpreter—the performer—takes second place.

The Great Guitars is a loose association of the jazz giants. From the left: Charlie Byrd, Herb Ellis, Barney Kessel.

The role of the composer is recorded in the history of music as a fact, while the role of the performer is regarded as ephemeral. The work remains; the performance, in time, will be forgotten. The names of famous virtuosi of the past become just a legend. This was true until modern technological development in sound recording. Now, a particular performance and an individual interpretation can be made permanent. An artist who has ended his concert career will no longer be the focus of public attention in the same way as the person who can still be seen in concert halls; but his or her recordings will continue to be valuable proof of their splendid art and a source of lasting enjoyment of music.

On the other hand, in the world of pop music the success of a composition depends on its presentation. Many songwriters remain virtually anonymous unless, of

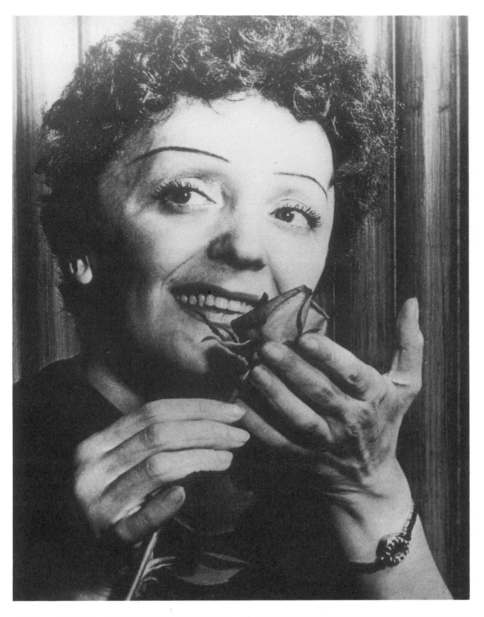

course, they are also the performers. It is the singing star, group, or occasionally, the instrumentalist who steals the limelight.

It is worth looking at some of the personalities who shone in the skies of pop music longer than the average. Indeed, some of them are still shining, even after decades, and have become living legends. But who should we choose? There are enough well-known names to fill an entire book, so let us put all their names into a hat and pull out a dozen or so.

Maurice Chevalier (1888–1972), elegant in evening dress and always carrying the essential straw hat, enchanted audiences in Paris and in the United States with his charm. The worldwide popularity of this performer, one of the greatest figures in French *chanson* popular singing, was boosted by Hollywood films and by *Gigi* in particular.

Non, je ne regrette rien ('No, I do not regret anything') is the unforgettable sentiment linked forever with the name of **Edith Piaf** (1915–63). A tiny woman of inconspicuous appearance, always dressed in black, she commanded a voice that sang the emotions of the ordinary person and the poetry of the streets of Paris. She became the 'Parisian Sparrow' *(Le piaf de Paris)* and few people remember that her real name was Edith Giovanna Gassion.

Marlene Dietrich (1901–92) was mainly known to the world as the singing star of some of the first Hollywood sound films. When the Fascist regime came to power in her native Germany, she asked for American citizenship. During

Edith Piaf at the time of her glory... and her final resting place in the Paris Père Lachaise cemetery.

Frank Sinatra

World War II she sang for the soldiers at the Front. Afterwards she returned to films. A careful study of her films suggests that she was rather better as a singer than as an actress, but she certainly possessed a truly magical and star-like quality.

Unlike many popular singers who have never had systematic

Yves Montand

Gilbert Bécaud

Charles Aznavour

Mireille Mathieu

The famous Moulin Rouge, Boulevard de Clichy, Paris.

Frank Zappa, singer, composer and music world businessman.

Italy is generally recognized as the cradle of magnificent singing. In the field of pop music, this is proved by the American singer **Frank Sinatra** (b. 1915), who inherited his musical gifts from his Italian parents. Sinatra started at a time when singers were only an accompaniment to swing bands, but audiences quickly and rightly started to turn their attention to him. In no time, his crooning voice made him a star of the first magnitude. In addition, he is a successful actor and an exceptionally prosperous businessman in the music industry.

Edith Piaf assisted a number of her younger colleagues in their international careers. One of them was **Charles Aznavour** (b. 1924), who with her assistance went out first to Canada and then to the United States. Aznavour's vocal qualities are not outstanding, but his melodies and lyrics and the manner of his delivery have won him audiences over several dec-

training in music, **Gilbert Bécaud** (b. 1927) was professionally trained as a composer—he studied at the conservatory in Nice — and a pianist. His songs have a well-planned musical construction. His performances captivate audiences through the content of his songs and through his singing and acting. He has also made a name for himself in the field of classical music as the composer of such pieces as *Christmas Oratorio*, *The Child and the Star* and *L'opera d'Aran*.

ades. In addition to performing, he is a successful businessman, being the owner of a publishing house and a concert agency. He is, in fact, from Armenia, his real name being Varenagh Aznavourian, and he was born in Paris. After the devastating earthquake in Armenia in 1988 he did not hesitate to go to help his homeland.

After Chevalier and Piaf and before Aznavour and Bécaud, **Yves Montand** (1921–91) was the biggest international star of the French chanson. Montand started as an amateur, singing songs from the repertoire of Maurice Chevalier. He performed in Edith Piaf's programme at the Moulin Rouge and was well received for his evening performances of recitals, repeated over a long period, in the Théâtre de l'Etoile and in the Olympia. He was made famous for all time by his songs *Les routiers* and *Le gamin de Paris.*

Without doubt, **Jacques Brel** (1929–78), the Belgian singer, poet and composer, belongs in the ranks of French chanson singers. His original way of performing and, above all, his view of the problems of the modern world and the challenging ideas he presented attracted a vast audience. There were times when he gave up to 300 performances a year and his records were sold by the millions. Despite such success, he gave up public performances to devote his time to composition. Later he withdrew completely from turbulent modern civilization to live out his life on a small island in the Pacific.

Mireille Mathieu (b. 1947) is sometimes looked upon as the successor to Edith Piaf. At 18 she won first prize in a local amateur contest and this was followed by an invitation to Paris to appear on television. This marked the begin-

ning of her career. Soon after, she was performing at the Olympia and made frequent tours abroad. She was particularly warmly welcomed in the United States. She appears constantly on French radio and TV. She excels in a brilliant singing technique and is known for her hard work.

One of the most important representatives of the rock era is undoubtedly the American **Frank Zappa** (b. 1940), singer, musician and composer. Zappa's work goes beyond the limitations of style and genre and incorporates jazz, rock and classical music, including electronics. At concert performances, his groups demonstrate a high standard of playing and also an unusual conception of stage direction, bringing in elements of the theatre. His music is exacting and the lyrics of his songs are serious in intent. Zappa is also the author of a number of films, which he

Elton John

Stevie Wonder

produces and successfully markets. He has always been among the top stars of world popularity.

If you visit Madame Tussaud's in London, you will find among the exhibits the singer **Elton John** (b. 1947), the first pop soloist to receive the honour of being immortalized as a wax figure. Elton John gained the honour through his lasting success with audiences, which he achieved through clever song-writing and the reliable quality of his performance.

His name is **Stevenland Judkins** (b. 1950) and he has been blind from birth. When he was 13, he made public appearances playing the mouth organ and singing with a pleasant, childish high-pitched voice. He was introduced as 'Little Stevie Wonder', and the name **Stevie Wonder** stuck. He has won a place among the most successful singers of our time. His songs, with their broad range of human interest, have won millions of admirers.

The European folk song and dance group has by no means been relegated to the museum yet, and is enjoying a revival.

Seeking the Sources

No one can escape from his or her past. We carry it within us, both as individuals and as whole societies. From time to time, we look into it more closely than usual, in order to rediscover values that can tell us something about ourselves, even today. This is true of many branches of human activity and it is also valid for music, including the field of pop music.

Folk songs, with their simple beauty and pure vision of the world, provide a strong contrast to the many negative influences of modern society. We still go back to the source for the folk songs that were part of the lives of our ancestors. The melodies of black spirituals have not faded and the lyrics of everyday life that originated centuries ago in all of the countries of Europe still have a lasting charm.

In most cases, folk songs no longer exist in their original form or in their original surroundings, which have also ceased to exist. These songs are now performed on stage—a welcome revival and a chance for us to look into the past. The songs are often played and sung by folk groups in their authentic form but, at the same time, they also take on a new shape. In modern arrangements, with modern instruments and quite often with rhythmic accompaniment, they sound similar to other types of modern pop music.

The revival of folk music has given rise to a powerful new wave of music that is derived from ancient roots but comments on the present day. Folk, western and country music share a similar and related content. The folk singer of today is no longer anonymous; his name is widely publicized and he

Joan Baez

Johnny Cash

thing around him. People listened to him outside circus tents, in barber shops and, later, on the radio. The most striking figure, of course, is **Bob Dylan** (b. 1941), whose real name is Robert Zimmermann. In Dylan's work, the poetic image alternates with commentary, between specific events of the present and images that reflect a younger generation's protest against an America of conservative, middle-class adults.

What about Tomorrow?

The development of pop music goes on. The streams of style change so rapidly that we can hardly keep track: punk, heavy metal; what will come after them?

The Renaissance period covered over 200 years; the Baroque lasted approximately 150 years; Classicism about 70 and Romanticism reigned for an entire century. The changes in style of classical music

Bob Dylan *(below)*

attracts large audiences. There are folk singers with guitars in coffee bars, student clubs and in pubs, and they perform on both small and large stages and at festivals. Sometimes their songs preserve the magic of traditional sound; at other times they present effective arrangements with modern bands. Two names, in particular, are of outstanding importance and influence in this field.

The American **Woody Guthrie** (1912–67) is considered by many to be the father of the modern folk movement. He was truly a folk singer, who gave voice out of an inner need to sing about every-

The piano, the classical instrument of large concert halls, also has its place in modern jazz.

took place slowly. Over a long period they were able to crystallize into works of lasting value. Epochs in the history of pop music may last 15 years, sometimes only five or ten, or even fewer. It is difficult to calculate how many trends and styles there have been in the development of jazz and pop music, how many were born and how many faded away to become just memories.

Interplanetary flight, the building of nuclear power stations or the construction of the Channel tunnel—all can be planned and a definite date set for the start, the finish and for the putting into operation. The development of the arts—even the art of entertainment—cannot be foretold. What today is considered wildly popular and attractive may be forgotten completely in a few years.

There is one thing, however, that persists: the ability of the human voice to convey ideas through words expressed in song, which can raise a smile, stimulate thought, recall happy moments or urge one to action. That is why singers have long competed with their colleagues—instrumentalists for the favour of audiences. And very often the singers are the winners.

Opera

To See and to Hear

She is a venerable old lady—she will soon celebrate her 400th birthday. She comes from Italy, where she was born in about 1600. For 200 years her language was exclusively Italian, and she learned very slowly to speak other languages. Despite her advanced age, she has not yet decided to give up because she still has much to offer. Over the years she has won more admirers throughout the world than any other branch of music. She has friends both on the stage and behind the scenes; those who create her, play, sing and dance her; she has millions of friends in many theatres who passionately admire her. She has become for them an essential part of life.

With advancing age she has changed, gained experience, grown older and then younger again. Above all, she is drama in song, but in the past she has sometimes abandoned her chief mission—to express dramatic action in music—and has revealed her other face: an opportunity for virtuoso singing.

A Dramatic Concert?

Opera is a complicated and expensive music form. Each production requires a large group to run it: singers, choir, orchestra, dancers occasionally and, of course, many

Opera developed at the end of the 16th century in Florence, in Italy.

A performance of Baroque opera on the stage of a castle theatre. The scenery and the singers' and musicians' costumes take us back 300 years. This is a scene from the opera *L'honeste negli amori* by Alessandro Scarlatti (1685–1757).

Above and right: **Operatic costumes from the time of Mozart.**

The technology of the 18th-century stage was unusually ingenious and complex, able to create surprising effects and make rapid changes of scenery. Characters appeared 'from the heavens' or disappeared through trapdoors. Boats sailed along the horizon and vehicles and animals appeared on the scene.

An old engraving of the coronation opera of J. J. Fux *Costanza e fortezza* praising Charles VI when he became King of Bohemia (Prague, 1723).

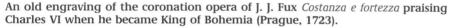

specialized professionals backstage.

At first, opera belonged exclusively to the pomp of the royal court or in the home of the aristocrat. Private Baroque theatres found in many mansions and palaces have quite small auditoriums because they were intended only for the family of the nobleman and his closest retainers. The stage, on the contrary, is spacious, as it was created to accommodate great spectacles. Opera was designed to dazzle its noble audience with its rich staging and unusual effects—which even included sea battles, fountains and waterfalls, light and sound-effects, characters hovering in the clouds or disappearing into an abyss, crowds of people, infantry and even mounted cavalry. At the same time, opera also entertained the audience with the virtuosity of its soloists.

Family celebrations in great houses—weddings, birthdays, visits of distinguished guests and, above all, coronations—were al-

ways an occasion for arranging magnificent operatic performances. One of the most spectacular took place in 1723, when a solemn opera was performed in Prague to mark the Bohemian coronation of the Austrian Emperor Charles VI. The Viennese court architect, Giuseppe Galli-Bibiena, erected an amphitheatre near Prague Castle to seat an audience of over 4,000, with a stage that was 63 metres (210 feet) deep, a space for an orchestra comprising 200 musicians and mechanical equipment that demonstrated the height of Baroque technical inventiveness.

The performance of the coronation opera of **Johann Joseph Fux** (1660–1741), *Costanza e fortezza* (Constancy and Strength), praising the ruler's virtues, lasted from eight in the evening until after midnight. The splendid structure, the costumes of the singers, the fountains and the stage illuminated by thousands of candles—all created a sight never before seen in Europe.

Ordinary people began to take an interest in this new musical style, and public theatres were soon built so that everyone who could pay an entrance fee could enjoy opera. The first opera house, Teatro San Cassiano, was opened in Venice in 1637.

Opera occupied such a place in people's lives at that time that television occupies in ours today. Over the course of a century the art of singing was perfected and

Right: **Designs for costumes for the characters of Leonora and Count Luna in Verdi's opera** *Il Trovatore.*

One of the most interesting opera houses in Europe, the Paris Opera, the work of architect Charles Garnier (1825–98). It was built in 1861–74.

The new Paris Opera.

people particularly admired the exceptional vocal virtuosity of *castrati* (men castrated before puberty so that their voices never broke). The singing style, called *bel canto* ('beautiful singing'), has never been surpassed. Hundreds of operas were written, some by composers of the first magnitude, such as Handel, others by hacks, who often repeated and reused themes and the same librettos. Popular librettos included those of the Italian poet Pietro Metastasio. His *Didone abbandonata* was set to music 60 times and *The Clemency of Titus* as many as 100 times. Audiences often knew the story in advance and went to the opera purely for the singing. Interest was centred on the arias, or solo parts, of the star singer, and minimal attention was paid to the prose linking the musical pieces.

Opera remained like this until the 1750s. After a while, the tragedy or drama of the serious performance, in which themes of antiquity predominated, began to be relieved by *intermezzi*, short comic operas inserted between the acts of *opera seria* (serious opera). If an opera had three acts, then a two-act intermezzo was played during the intervals. Later, the *opera buffa* (comic opera) developed from the intermezzo. The first such work was *La serva padrona* ('The Maid as Mistress') composed by **Giovanni Battista Pergolesi** (1710–36), which was performed in Naples in 1733. This work of historical importance, presenting a simple, contemporary, story, determined for many decades the rule that there should be two acts in all comic operas.

A reaction to virtuoso singing, which some saw as suppressing dramatic truth, was *Orfeo ed Euridice* (1762), the unconventional, 'reforming' opera of Gluck. In this work the art returned to its original intention—to present the dramatic story truthfully.

Cathedrals of the Arts

Opera houses became the secular counterparts of cathedrals. They achieved this both externally—in their monumental architecture—and internally—in that human experiences was brought to life, together with the ideas, sentiments and aspirations of the times. This was brought about by combining several branches of the arts—literature, visual art, drama, music and dance.

Each opera house has its own story to tell. In each you will find the life histories of the operas performed there and of the personalities, victories and failures connected with them. They chronicle the premières received with applause and the performances that were booed, the struggles to establish important ideals and the petty quarrels behind the scenes.

Mozart in Prague

Mozart did not have things easy in Vienna, so he was glad to accept an invitation from his friends in Prague to visit their city where his *Le nozze di Figaro* ('The Marriage of Figaro') was currently being performed with great success. When he stepped from the coach into the January frosts of 1787 after a three-day journey, he was surprised to discover that Prague was

Wolfgang Amadeus Mozart

Above: **The Bertramka Villa in Prague, where Mozart finished his opera** *Don Giovanni* **in 1787.**

Left: **The Estates Theatre in Prague, dedicated to 'Patriae et Musis'—the Homeland and the Muses—as the golden inscription on the front proclaims. The first performance of Mozart's opera** *Don Giovanni* **was given here, with the composer himself conducting.**

61

alive with his music. People in the streets were singing and whistling melodies from his operas, especially Figaro's Act I aria 'Non più andrai'. His music was being played by wandering harpists in the taverns, and at balls, people were whirling in German dance style to arrangements of his music from *Figaro*.

Mozart stayed with his friends the Dušeks in the Bertramka Villa outside Prague. Josefina Dušková was an excellent singer and her husband, the composer František Xaver Dušek, enjoyed the favour of Prague society as a well-patronized music teacher. Mozart was invited to the salons of the nobility and lionized as a splendid virtuoso pianist. He conducted a performance of his *Symphony in D major*, which was popularly known as the *Prague Symphony*. Naturally, he also conducted a performance of *The Marriage of Figaro*.

Mozart's visit was a sensation; he was showered with attention and praise by everyone.

'My orchestra is in Prague,' he declared when he discovered the excellent standard of the Prague theatre orchestra. And as for the audiences, he is said to have commented approvingly, 'My Prague people understand me.' He was happy to promise a new opera for the city's theatre.

Mozart revisited Prague at the end of the summer of the same year, bringing with him the almost completed score of *Don Giovanni*. Is it true that Mozart wrote the overture the night before

Left, above: **A statue of Mozart in Vienna.**

Madamina, il catalogo e questo . . . **Don Giovanni's servant Leporello presents Donna Elvira with a list of the loves of his master.**

the première? That is what legend says. The opera was prepared, rehearsed and, because of various obstacles, its performance had to be deferred. The day of the première was fixed, but Mozart still did not have an overture. It is said that he sat at his desk the night before the memorable performance, with his quill racing across the paper. While he was working, his wife Constance told him fairy-tales. Copyists arrived in the morning to write out the parts for the various instuments to play that evening.

Can we believe the legend? In part. Mozart often composed his music in his mind long before he wrote down the first note; his brain worked like a perfect computer. Recording the notes on paper was just a mechanical matter for such a composer. But could the orchestra, though very skilful, play a complicated composition from a score at first sight without rehearsal? This part of the legend is difficult to believe.

The success of the première of *Don Giovanni* on 29 October, 1787, exceeded all expectations. The libretto was in Italian, but the audience understood; they knew the story beforehand. Mozart, who conducted the first performance, was given an ovation.

Four years later, in 1791, Mozart was commissioned to write a serious opera—*La Clemenza di Tito* ('The Clemency of Titus') — for the coronation of Emperor Leopold. This time, the citizens of Prague did not get to the theatre to welcome their maestro once again. The auditorium was filled with the aristocracy and members of the court. 'German trash,' declared the Empress, the Spanish Infanta Maria Ludovica, and this sealed the opera's fate. Although it had an Italian libretto, it was markedly different in style from the Italian operas that were then customary. Its failure embittered the last act of Mozart's life.

A Flop

One might have encountered almost anything at the opera

Right, above: **A scene from** *Il barbiere di Siviglia*, **an opera by Gioacchino Rossini.**

A medieval castle in a painting by Antonín Mánes (1784–1843) introduces the chapter on Romantic opera. Music and the visual arts are different media but their content is often related.

The Schauspielhaus (now the Konzerthaus) in Berlin presented the gala première of Weber's *Der Freischütz* in 1821.

A scene from Weber's *Der Freischütz*.

house, especially in Italy. Popular arias were applauded enthusiastically—sometimes they had to be repeated as many as three times—people talked aloud during the performance, now and then shouting at the performers, and the audience often whistled or stamped their feet when their views differed from those of the composer or the conductor.

There was an extraordinary scandal in Rome in 1816 during the première of **Gioacchino Antonio Rossini's** (1792–1868) *Il barbiere di Siviglia* ('The Barber of Seville'). The figure of the wily servant Figaro, as we know him from Mozart's opera based on a play by Pierre Beaumarchais, appears in other plays by the same author. 'The Barber' had already been set to music by the composer **Giovanni Paisiello** (1740–1816), 34 years previously. He saw to it that the young composer was properly cut down to size. Paisiello had no difficulty in bribing a part of the audience, called the *claque*, to create a disturbance. (This used to be done quite frequently.) In addition, there were one or two mishaps on the stage and the première of Rossini's opera was turned into a flagrant scandal. Rossini was a calm person, however, and did not allow himself to be upset. After the performance, he went home and slept tranquilly.

The next day, the tide changed and 'The Barber' celebrated an unexpected triumph. Since then, it has been performed at opera houses throughout the world — and always to full houses. The ever-brisk humour always provokes ripples of laughter, and the wit and cleverness of the music always reap enthusiastic applause.

Rossini was an unusually prolific composer, although malicious

Carl Maria von Weber

Richard Wagner

tongues claim that he was lazy (more stories are told about his enjoyment of cooking and culinary skills then about his ability as a composer). In 20 years—from the age of 17 to 37—Rossini wrote 39 operas, sometimes composing four or even six in a single year. Two of them earned him immense popularity, 'The Barber' and *Guillaume Tell* ('William Tell'), the latter based on Friedrich Schiller's play about a well-known Swiss hero. The 'William Tell' overture and the overtures to *La gazza lada* ('The Thieving Magpie') and *La scata diseta* ('The Silken Ladder') are perennially popular concert pieces.

Rossini's works, which were strongly influenced by Mozart, continued in the best tradition of the Italian comic *opera buffa* and required that the singers were at their peak.

Mystery and Romanticism

Let us now leave the sun-drenched south and set out for the north, to the opera houses of Germany.

The curtain goes up and on the darkened stage we see the mysterious wolf's glen. It is just midnight and the young huntsman Kasper, who has sold his soul to the Devil, is calling up the devil Samiel within a magic circle. He is asking for help in moulding seven magic bullets. The forces of Hell are to guide the shots of his rival Max and the last of them should reach Agathe, Max's bride-to-be. The fire flares up, the voices of spectres sound, lightning crisscrosses the sky. We hold our breath. This is a scene from the opera *Der Freischütz* ('The Marksman', 1821), in which we are told a story that is half folklore and half true. It was composed by **Carl Maria von Weber** (1786–1826).

In contrast to previous operas, Weber's *Der Freischütz* presents an entirely new world, both in its theme and in its technique. The characters are ordinary people and the setting is countryside, not a palace or the salon of an aristocrat. The singing is not in Italian but in a language the audience understands. The orchestra is not limited to accompaniment, but

Important opera houses in Europe

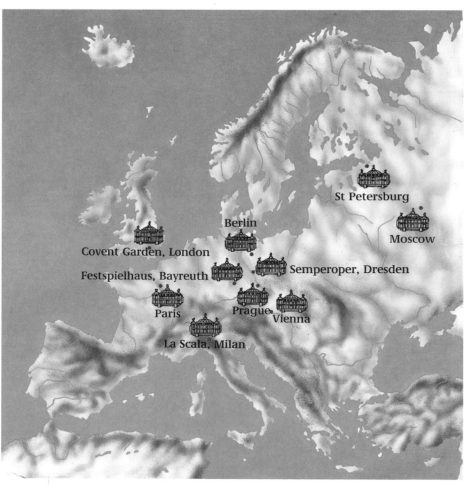

Scene from Verdi's opera *Aida*.

The composer had special trumpets made for *Aida*.

Two later operas, *Euryanthe* and *Oberon*, further developed the principle of Romantic opera. They also set the pattern for Germany's greatest operatic composer, Richard Wagner.

Between Germany and Italy

Germany and Italy experienced similar fates in the 19th century; their countries were divided up into small states, even though the people spoke the same language and had common interests. People longed for their countries to be unified and for the establishment of a republican political system.

Giuseppe Verdi

describes the environment and gives colour to the action. He introduces sound effects—deep and sombre strings, clarinets and French horns lead us into romantic forests.

The première of the opera took place in Berlin, and it was the first opera performance in the newly opened Schauspielhaus on Gendarmenmarkt (today it is the Platz der Akademie in Berlin). The theatre has been renamed Konzerthaus.

Both opera and composer were a triumphant success. *Der Freischütz* marked the start of Romanticism in opera and a new dominance for German opera as opposed to Italian. Weber's work, harmonizing with the aspirations of the young generation in Germany at the beginning of the 19th century, also played its role in the advance of national consciousness, and not in Germany alone.

Apart from his work as a composer, Weber was also a piano virtuoso. Among other things, he wrote two piano concertos, four piano sonatas, and a popular waltz fantasy, 'Invitation to the Dance', with instrumentation by Hector Berlioz. Between 1813 and 1816 Weber was conductor of the German opera in Prague, and in

Groups of people of the same mind striving for this end called themselves Young Germany and Young Italy.

Both countries found the expression of their desire for unification in the works of two great opera composers—Giuseppe Verdi and Richard Wagner. Indeed, the opera house became a meeting place where it was possible to express

Left: **The Opera House in Bayreuth, designed for performances of Richard Wagner's operas, is the setting of important music festivals every year.**

Below: La Dame aux camélias, **a novel by Alexandre Dumas, was the subject of Verdi's opera *La Traviata*. In a later dramatic performance of the work, the lead was played by the French actress Sarah Bernhardt. The Art Nouveau poster is the work of the Czech artist Alfons Mucha (1860–1939).**

Traviata—were written in the early 1850s. *Un ballo in maschera* ('A Masked Ball'), *La forza del destino* ('The Force of Destiny') and *Don Carlos* followed. Considerable attention was aroused by *Aida*, com-

agreement or disagreement both with the opera and with ideas it expressed. Artistic form influenced public opinion and aroused nationalist feelings; opera had an importance equal to that of modern cinema or television.

'Fly, thought, on golden wings'

Giuseppe Verdi (1813–1901) was not accepted by Milan Conservatorio on the grounds that he lacked talent. Even so, he became one of the greatest Italian composers of all times. The traditional Italian gift for singing and the continuous interest of ordinary people in the theatre were concentrated in his works, whose themes harmonized with the sentiments of Italian society at that time.

After a shaky start and the failure of his second opera, Verdi was reluctant to continue composing. A friend, however, insisted on giving him a libretto for a new opera. Once at home, Verdi threw it irritably on to the table. The book opened by chance at a page carrying the text of a song: *Va, pensiero, sull'ali dorate . . .* ('Fly, thought, on golden wings . . .'). Verdi started reading the verses and at once became absorbed in the theme—the liberation of the Jews from Babylonian captivity. He set to work immediately and within a few months, wrote the opera *Nabucco* (1842). The song of the downtrodden, the theme of independence and the use of ordinary people on the stage—together with Verdi's easy-to-sing music and masterly structuring of the action—suited both the performers and the audience. The première was a triumph such as the La Scala in Milan had not seen for many years. Verdi became the idol of Italy. The chorus 'Fly, thought, on golden wings . . .' was sung as the anthem of the Italian patriots.

More operas followed and their melodies were sung by the people on their way from the theatre. They were played by organ grinders in the streets and on melodeons in bars. Verdi wrote 25 operas in all. Three of the best known— *Rigoletto, Il Trovatore* and *La*

missioned by the Egyptian government for the opening ceremony of the Suez Canal in 1871. In his last two operas, *Otello* (1887) and *Falstaff* (1893), based on Shakespearean characters, Verdi shows the influence of his great contemporary, **Richard Wagner** (1813—83).

Music and Drama

On a hill above the Bavarian town Bayreuth stands a theatre. It is plain brick and not very impressive, but it is unique. It is the only building in the world used solely for the performance of the operas by one composer.

In the summer of 1876, audiences saw the first staging of the cycle of Richard Wagner's four operas, *Der Ring des Nibelungen*

Ema Destinová (Emmy Destinn), the famous dramatic singer at the beginning of the 20th century.

('The Ring of Nibelung', or simply 'The Ring'). This took place on four evenings in Bayreuth. A festival of Wagner's works, to which some of the best musicians in the world are invited, is held in Bayreuth every year. It is a festival not only of German culture, but of the entire world of music.

In his works, Richard Wagner personified the idea of German patriotism as it developed in the first half of the 19th century. He encapsulated the cult of Teutonic heroes and mythology, which received a great deal of attention during the period when efforts were being made to unify Germany. Wagner's musical drama aimed at

A scene from Giacomo Puccini's opera *Madame Butterfly*.

Placido Domingo, one of the current stars in the operatic sky.

the idea of *Gesamtkunstwerk*, to combine all of the arts together in a balanced unit. In his operas, the difference between an aria and a recitative disappeared completely; the stream of the music was carried along in continuous melody that fitted easily with the poetic text. Wagner was the author of his own librettos. He also participated in the direction of the production and stage settings of each opera.

'Laugh, Clown, Laugh'

The dominance of Romanticism in art ended as the new century approached. The era of decadence demanded new impulses. People no longer wanted to be presented with a dream world, but with the actual world in which they were living. They wanted to meet themselves in works of art. They read the novels of Emile Zola, and went to see the plays of Henrik Ibsen. A new style appeared in the visual arts, Art Nouveau. In Paris, Alfons Mucha was designing stage settings and posters for Sarah Bernhardt, the greatest French actress of that time. Her most famous role was in Dumas's *La Dame aux camélias*, which Giuseppe Verdi had made famous in his opera, *La Traviata*.

In the opera house, too, contemporary figures were appearing; people of flesh and blood—*di carne e d'ossa*, as it was described in the prologue to the opera *I Pagliacci* ('The Clowns') by **Ruggiero Leoncavallo** (1858–1919). This was a play within a play; the fate of the characters in the comedy intermingles with the fate of real people. The story is about love, jealousy and violent passion and it ends in tragedy. In the famous aria, the Ringmaster Canio sings: '. . . The people pay for their seats and want to laugh, If Harlequin seduces your Columbine, Laugh, clown, as they applaud, laugh.'

I Pagliacci, together with **Pietro Mascagni**'s (1863–1945) *Cavalleria rusticana*, telling the story of a Sicilian village, heralded a new trend in the world of opera—*verismo*, meaning realism. Although both composers wrote many more operas, these one-act operas, produced at the outset of their careers, brought them lasting fame.

They are usually performed together in a single evening.

The third and best-known of the famous trio of verismo composers was **Giacomo Puccini** (1858–1924). His *La Bohème* (1896) takes us among the artists and seamstresses of Paris. *Tosca* (1900) is full of dramatic passion, while *Madame Butterfly* (1904) tells the story of the unrequited love of a Japanese geisha girl for an American naval officer. *Turandot* (finished after his death in 1926) is staged in the exotic surroundings of old China.

Verismo was to opera what naturalism was to literature. Realism and truth above all were the principle. In these operas we hear a persistant melody, simple harmony and sharp sound contrasts that are close to Italian folk melodies. Above all, *verismo* provided an opportunity to make use of the beauty of the human voice.

Wagner's Heir

The development of German Romantic opera, starting with Weber's *Freischütz* and culminating in the Neo-Romantic art of Richard Wagner, reached its peak with the work of **Richard Strauss** (1864–1949).

At a time when Italy was pouring a wave of *verismo* into the world, Strauss was composing work in Germany that were continuing to develop the principles of musical drama started by Wagner. His two full-length, one-act operas return us to a Biblical figure in

The family of operatic artists includes the stage designer. In his studio, he starts by planning the layout of the stage, first of all as a sketch, then as a three-dimensional model.

Salome (1905), and to antiquity in *Electra* (1909), although in both cases, the main purpose is to depict human characters, to present the drama of personalities and the clash between them.

Strauss made use of the sound effects possible with a large symphony orchestra; he also made exacting demands on the voices of the singers. His next two operas, however, showed a completely new outlook and technique. He set his sights on the society of imperial Vienna at the time of Maria Theresa and wrote *Der Rosenkavalier* (1911). Nevertheless, he does not characterize the period and the environment by using music reminiscent of the mid-18th century, as could have been expected, but shaped the opera as a great waltz fantasy. Another of his works is the cheerful, intimate opera *Ariadne auf Naxos*, in which ancient Greek drama is intermingled with *commedia dell'arte* foolery.

New Roads

Pessimists frequently prophesy that opera will soon be singing its swan song; its development has finished, all possibilities have been exhausted, it is out of the question to go on. It has repeatedly been shown that this is not so.

The audience also has a hand in the development of opera and this changes, too, as the world changes. It is true that many of the ideas in famous operas of past eras no longer harmonize with our way of thinking. Endless arias do not correspond with the frantic tempo of modern life. The complicated plots of comedies, routinely written according to a well-tried recipe, have survived, although we are aware that their librettos were, even in their own time, mostly an excuse for many composers to write brilliant music.

Despite these objections, we shall never cease to admire the beauty of the human voice. We shall continue going to the opera to relish the glory of the great stars' voices. And we shall also always ponder on mankind's eternal ideals, on the relationships be-

Left, above: **The Schönbrunn Castle calls to mind the glorious era of imperial Vienna in the mid-18th century. It was where Richard Strauss set his opera** *Der Rosenkavalier.*

Left, below: **The National Theatre in Prague. A substantial part of its operatic repertoire comprises the works of Bedřich Smetana, Antonín Dvořák, Leoš Janáček and Bohuslav Martinů.**

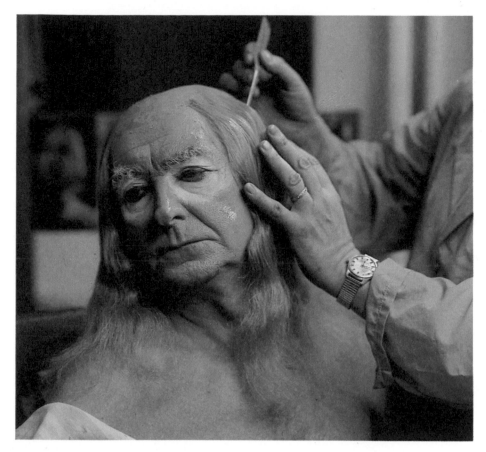

The curtain goes up in an hour. In the dressing room, the soloist is in the hands of the make-up artist, who will turn him into the Water Sprite for Dvořák's opera *Rusalka.*

tween people and on the spiritual wealth invested in their works by the great masters of times gone by.

But time has not stood still, even in the opera house. The language of music has changed, as well as the concept of operatic performance. Opera has grown closer to drama, ballet, the musical and often to film as well. Stage sets are making use of modern technical innovations—lighting, sound and other techniques to enhance the staging and to give opera a new form. Like audiences in the past, we, too, admire the beautifully sung phrase, but we also demand the ability to hear and understand the words. Modern electro-acoustic equipment is able to meet this requirement as well.

The Stage Resounds With Dance

How many ballet shoes does a dancer wear out in one season?

It Started in France

Each country has contributed something to the world of music— the waltz was born in Vienna, jazz in the United States, opera in Italy and ballet in France. Even before the first opera was performed in Florence, ballet was a part of the spectacular festivities taking place at the French court. It reached its first peak during the reign of the Sun King Louis XIV (1643–1715).

King Louis XIV
in the Sun costume.

French society enjoyed dancing in the Louvre and at Versailles, and the splendid costumes and elegant movements of the dancers were a feast for the eyes.

While opera required the singers and musicians to be specially trained, anyone could dance without needing lengthy instruction. The King himself loved to dance. He appeared in a ballet production when he was 15 years old, wearing the Sun costume, and he was always referred to afterwards as *Le Roi Soleil* ('The Sun King'). At the time, there were several hundred dancing masters in Paris, but only a few of them enjoyed the King's favour. In order to give the noble art of the dance a system and bring it to the height of perfection, King Louis founded L'Académie Royale de Dance in Paris for the training of dance masters.

The rigidity of court ballet, restricted by cumbersome costumes, was somewhat changed by the royal court bandmaster and composer **Jean-Baptiste Lully** (1632–87). He introduced a livelier tempo into ballet music, forcing the dancers to make more rapid and relaxed movements. Ballet shifted from the dance-hall to the stage, either as part of an opera or as an independent dance production.

Balletic interludes became an essential part of Baroque opera. They supported the opera's story, but also provided vivid entertain-

ment and so became unusually popular. The stage was filled with dozens of male and female dancers. Sometimes the effect was heightened by the introduction of trained animals.

Ballet has, to some extent, retained its place in opera even in modern times. It was a usual part of many romantic operas, such as the dancing in the operas of Pyotr Ilyich Tchaikovsky, in **Charles Gounod**'s (1818–93) *Faust*, the *Polovtsian Dances* in **Alexander Borodin**'s (1833–87) *Prince Igor*, and the dancing in Bedřich Smetana's (1824–84) operas.

It took a long time for ballet to extract itself completely from rigid conventions and to become a musical and dramatic work in which a story is expressed through movement and music. This did not come about until the 19th century. The basic impulse for this came from the important French choreographer **Jean Georges Noverre** (1727–1810), who set down the basics for the ballet of action.

From France to Russia

In the first half of the 19th century France still held the top position in the art of ballet. France put on the stage the first Romantic ballet, *La Sylphide* (1832), to music by the composer **Jean Schneitzhoeffer**, followed by *Giselle* (1841), based on the theme by Théophile Gautier and set to music by **Adolphe Charles Adam** (1803–56). Classical technique, especially in the female dancers, reached astonishing virtuosity, their movements seem-

Left, above: **Versailles, the seat of French kings, was fertile soil for the blossoming of all branches of the arts.**

Left: La Sylphide, **a 19th-century Romantic ballet, is still able to fill the auditorium.**

ing to deny the earth's gravity. Sylphide, an ethereal fairy, was portrayed by Maria Taglioni, who danced on her toes for the first time, seeming to drift lightly above the ground. The music of Romantic ballet is based on a set libretto and the composer works in close co-operation with the choreographer. Ballet separated from opera, to be only an occasional guest in future.

In Western Europe ballet did not keep pace with the development of the Neo-Romantic dramatic arts, personified by Richard Wagner. The centre of its evolution shifted to Russia, where the mature art of the dance was taken by French artists. They were welcomed at the court of the Tsar, especially the choreographer **Marius Petipa** (1818–1910).

In France, the popular *Coppélia*

(1870) was written with music by **Léo Delibes** (1836–91); but after that, the best ballets were born in Moscow and St Petersburg. Above all, Russia had **Tchaikovsky**, who wrote ballet scores of lasting value, including *Swan Lake* (1877), *The Sleeping Beauty* (1890) and *The Nutcracker Suite* (1892). Even so, the influence of France, the cradle of ballet, still remains. For example, throughout the world ballet still uses French terminology.

Russia Conquers Paris

Cultural relations between France and Russia were strong at this time. A knowledge of French was part of a Russian aristocrat's education and the French were popular companions and tutors in aristocratic residences. This is exemplified, for instance, by the delightful Monsieur Triquet, the well-known figure in Tchaikovsky's opera *Eugene Onegin*. The Russian aristocrat Lady von Meck, who supported Tchaikovsky, also became the benefactress of Claude Debussy. Visits by Russian artists to Paris, where at the turn of the century there was a rich cultural life, provided great inspiration for Russian art.

The polymath **Sergey Pavlovich Diaghilev** (1872–1929), writer, connoisseur, and entrepreneur, arranged a very successful exhibition of Russian paintings in Paris in 1906. After that he organized a concert of Russian music and presented Paris with the opera *Boris Godunov* by **Modest Petrovich Mussorgsky** (1839–81) with

Left, above: **A scene from** *Giselle.*

Left: **The most popular ballet of the 19th century was** *Swan Lake,* **danced to the wonderful music of Pyotr Ilyich Tchaikovsky.**

Pyotr Ilyich Tchaikovsky

Right: '**Theatre of Living Figures**' is the inscription on the fair booth where the story of the clown Petrushka is told in Stravinsky's ballet.

Right, below: **Romeo and Juliet**—a scene from Sergey Prokofiev's ballet.

the fine bass singer **Fyodor Chaliapin** (1873–1933).

The French were very interested in Russian art. Diaghilev soon put together a group of Russian ballet dancers, Les Ballets Russes, headed by the choreographer and ballet master **Mikhail Fokin** (1880–1942). They staged remarkable ballet performances every year. They presented, for instance, Borodin's the *Polovtsian Dances*, the symphonic suite *Sheherazade* by **Nikolay Rimsky-Korsakov** (1844–1908), the ballet *Les Sylphides* to the music of Chopin, and later, Debussy's symphonic poem *Prélude à l'après-midi d'un faune*.

The main principle of S. P. Diaghilev's company was to link together the musical, creative and dance components on an equal level. While the technique of classical ballet meant essential training for all the dancers, this was by no means their aim; it was mainly the music that determined the

The rich movement of dance has been captured in many paintings and sculptures by Edgar Degas.

manner of expression through movement. The group selected compositions that had not originally been intended for dancing, the music and ideological content inspiring them to interpretation through dance.

The Ballets Russes quickly won the co-operation of **Igor Stravinsky** (1882–1971), one of the greatest Russian composers of this cen- tury, and later that of the young **Sergey Prokofiev** (1891–1953). Stravinsky's ballet *The Fire Bird*, first staged at the Paris Opera House, marked another important step in the success of Russian bal- let. This was followed by *Petrushka* (1911), a lively depiction of a Russian fair, with folk characters and the immortal tragi-comic clown—the Russian folklore equiv-

The five positions of the feet are the basis of classical dance.

alent of the Italian Purchinello or the French Polichinelle.

Another of Stravinsky's major works was *The Rite of Spring* (1913), with scenes from pagan society and music with clashing tonality and revolutionary percussive rhythms. It was so unusual that it aroused noisy protest in the auditorium. We know today that on the evening of its première, the Russian ballet and Stravinsky's music were pointing far into the future in the development of the arts of both dancing and music.

The corps, or main body of dancers of the Ballet Russes was filled with splendid performers. One of them, Anna Pavlova, won fame as a soloist for her interpretation of the *Dying Swan* to the music of **Camille Saint-Saëns** (1835–1921).

The Continuing Past

In the former USSR, too, the art of ballet followed the road taken by its Russian predecessors. Soviet composers created a number of remarkable full-length ballets. These include **Boris Asafiev** (1884–1949), composer of *The Flames of Paris* (1932) and *Bakhchisarai Fountain* (1934); the Armenian composer **Aram Khachaturian** (1903–78) wrote *Gayaneh* (1942) and *Spartacus* (1956); and **Sergey Prokofiev**, who enriched modern classical ballet with his *Romeo and Juliet* (1938), *Cinderella* (1945), and *The Stone Flower* (1954).

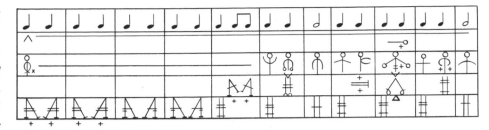

One way of making a graphic record of dance movement.

Into the Present

As music developed, so did the art of ballet. Generally speaking, modern music still uses acoustic theory developed centuries ago. It has at its disposal musical tones that have come about through the division of the octave into 12 equal intervals. However, these sounds are enriched by new instruments, and at its most progressive, music replaces the existing tone with new electronic sounds.

A similar situation exists in the basics of classical dance. The techniques of ballet still depends on the five positions of the feet and arms, the basic steps and their combinations, the jumps and the turns. In parallel with the development of new sounds, ballet also looks for new means of expression and new kinds of expressive movement. As music expresses ideas, relationships and stories through the sounds of musical instruments, so ballet does through movement.

Wanted
An inventor who will devise reliable and easy-to-read characters

for recording dance movements. They should express movements for solo dancers, their partners and the entire corps de ballet. They should also express all movement in relation to the stage area. In the manner of musical score, they must record the course of the whole ballet performance so that, even years later, the entire composition can be recreated in unchanged form. Motto: The ephemeral art of the moment.

Today this advertisement would probably get very few replies. There have been plenty of inventors who have attempted, with more or less success, to capture on paper the unusually intricate movements representing the art of dance.

To this day, dance 'characters' are more a support fot the memory just like the first musical notations. Choreographers have always used schematic drawings and written descriptions. Now, however, papers covered with sketches and written instructions are being replaced by video cameras, which are more reliable and more precise.

The Comic Theatre

Comedians and Buffoons

It would be foolish to smash a mirror just because it shows us how we really look or because it is slightly distorting, even if it gives us large noses and donkey's ears. Rather, we should laugh at ourselves and invite our friends to take a look as well.

Holding up a mirror in the theatre has always been the prerogative of jesters and clowns; they were permitted to say things to their masters that no one else would dare to—and they were even applauded for it.

In the Italian people's theatre, the *commedia dell'arte,* both powerful and ordinary people were introduced to their good and bad features. Comedy created firmly established figures drawn from life. It brought on to the scene the rich merchant Pantaloon, the clever servant Harlequin, the loving Colombine, the comic, luckless Pierrot and a large number of other types and their off-shoots. Such comic figures found their way to the operatic scene, for instance Ruggiero Leoncavallo's (1858–1919) *Pagliacci.* We still meet them in various guises on the stage and on the screen.

Songs are a part of comic theatre. They emphasize the dialogue and complete or stress things which have only been hinted at. Songs slow down the action if there is a need for thought or when the stage set is being changed. They bring the act to its culmination with a spectacular finish. Songs, arias, couplets, duets— these are some of the forms that make up musical comedy. All the different types are related, whether a fairground farce, a German *Singspiel,* an Italian *opera buffa,* French *opéra comique,* English ballad opera, French *vaudeville,* Parisian or Viennese *operetta* or an American musical.

Parody

A preponderance of Baroque opera, with its mythical heroes and powerful rulers, created a need to look at life from the other, somewhat brighter side. For example, it seemed a good idea to make fun of the mannerisms of contemporary theatre and to speak and sing in a language the audience could understand and not only in Italian.

The first parody on serious

The artist has depicted various figures from Italian comedy on the walls of the carnival hall.

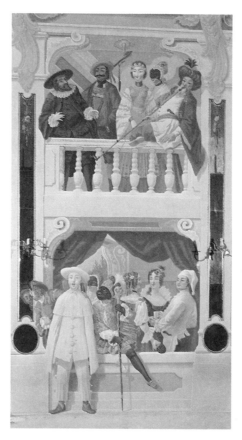

The Beggar's Opera **in a modern staging and adaptation by Benjamin Britten.**

opera was written in England. In 1728, *The Beggar's Opera* was performed in a London theatre in Lincoln's Inn Fields. The music was composed by **Johann Christoph Pepusch** (1667–1752) with a libretto by John Gay (1685–1732). It became the main attraction of the London theatre season. The opera contained allusions to political events, as well as conditions in the theatre, vulgar songs were sung, as well as the melodies of

respected composers, such as Handel, who was then the main representative of serious Italian opera in England. This 'noble' music was performed by characters from the lowest level of society, from whom a gentleman should always keep his dignified distance. Even so, *The Beggar's Opera* was a success. During two seasons, it was performed over 100 times and opened the way for comedy on the operatic stage.

Singspiel

At a time when Italian operatic *staggiones,* travelling groups of actors and singers, were performing in most European theatres, Vienna had its own people's theatre. There, performances were given in German in tandem with the official performances for high society. These were farces with songs, or *singspiels*, which contrasted with the seriousness of

chitect Charles Garnier and one of the most beautiful theatres in Europe—Paris had about 30 professional theatres. The city had a population of one-and-a-half million. It enjoyed a mixed cultural and social life and set the tone for the rest of Europe. France was experiencing years of prosperity; it had reason to boast to the world of its industry, technology and culture. That is why it planned the first World Exhibition in 1855.

It was at this time that a new type of theatre performance,

Italian opera. They featured figures from folklore, the most popular being the wise jester Hanswurst. *Singspiels* contained a great deal of singing, including simple folk songs, in the performance. Gradually, however, the musical component was intensified to take on a more serious element. This was helped along by Mozart's operas—*singspiels* based on German texts—such as the capricious *The Abduction from the Seraglio* (1782), and his last opera, *The Magic Flute* (1791). Mozart wrote it for

the fringe theatre, basing it on a libretto by the theatre's manager, Emanuel Schikaneder.

The Operetta

With the Second Empire, Paris became a modern city. Its medieval ground-plan was criss-crossed by a network of broad boulevards, and a town hall, palaces, department stores, railway stations, banks, market-places and theatres were built. In addition to the Opera House—the work of the ar-

called *Bouffes Parisiens,* was born in a small wooden theatre on the Champs-Elysées, not far from the Exhibition palaces. It was a cheerful, musical theatre, which had not set itself any other aim but entertaining theatre-goers. Father of the theatre was the German band-master, composer and businessman **Jacques Offenbach** (1819–80). He was the creator of a new type of comic opera, related to the Italian *opera buffa.* Unlike *opera buffa,* Offenbach's theatre included spoken dialogue. Later, the now universal name operetta (little opera), caught on. After his first success, Offenbach wrote one operetta after another, some were one act long, some full-length. He described them as comic opera, *bouffonerie* and *opera buffa.* He wrote almost 100 operettas. Inside his theatre, in rich settings, performers spoke, sang and danced. The audience roared with laughter, applauded the clever dialogue, the unusual situations and the lovely singing.

Three years after opening the Bouffes Parisiens Theatre, Offenbach staged his most famous work, the operetta *Orpheus in the Underworld,* an ancient theme in modern style. In this version of the story, the legendary singer Orpheus is director of a conservatoire, and Eurydice becomes his flighty wife, allowing herself to be kidnapped by Pluto, the ruler of Hell. The original legend was turned upside down and accompanied by plenty of beautiful, easily digestible music, including

the famous cancan. A few years later, Offenbach wrote *La Belle Hélène* ('Beautiful Helen'), which tells the story, in a rather strange manner, of what led up to the Trojan War.

Offenbach had both rivals and followers. One outstanding example was **Florimond Hervé** (1825–92) and his evergreen operetta *Mamzelle Nitouche* (1883)

The City on the Danube

It was not long before the Austrian metropolis, the city that 50 years earlier had set all Europe dancing to the rhythm of the waltz, responded to Offenbach's operettas. Vienna had always had a feeling for good entertainment, ranging from people's theatres to the official culture of the Imperial

Right, above: **Offenbach's most famous operetta is, without doubt,** *Orpheus in the Underworld.*

Right: Mamzelle Nitouche, **Florimond Hervé's operetta, has survived to this day and is still popular.**

court. It is not surprising that the sounds coming from Paris found a welcoming echo in Vienna.

The Parisian music was caught by the composer **Franz von Suppé** (1819–95), who started to develop a Viennese style. He became famous for his operetta *The Beautiful Galathea* and for *The Light Cavalry*, the overture of which is now one of the most popular pieces in concert repertoires. There is, of course, another composer whose name is permanently linked with Vienna, the town on the beautiful blue Danube. That is **Johann Strauss the Younger**. Until then, Strauss had been known and respected mainly as king of the waltz, but he, too, fell to the charm of the operetta and stands alongside Offenbach as one of its best-known composers.

Strauss's operettas were modelled to the taste of his Viennese audiences and the melody of the waltz, which was an inseparable part of Viennese local colour, naturally played a substantial role in the musical content. His operettas were carried from the ballrooms to the stages of the theatres. Strauss wrote 16 operettas, of which the best known, and still performed, are *Die Fledermaus* ('The Bat') and *Der Zigeunerbaron* ('The Gipsy Baron').

The example and successes of the two composers Suppé and Strauss led to the composition of more operettas, such as those by the composers **Carl Millöcker** (1842–99) and **Carl Zeller** (1842–98). They could not equal Strauss or Suppé, but they helped to fill the golden age of the Viennese operetta.

At the beginning of the 20th century, the composer **Franz Lehar** (1870–1948) shone with brilliance, with the operettas *The Count of Luxembourg* (1909), *Gipsy Love* (1910), *Frasquita* (1922) and the ever-popular *Merry Widow* (1905). Also, the composers **Oscar Straus** (1870–1954) and **Leo Fall** (1873–1925) gained popularity. They were joined by the Czech composer and conductor **Oskar Nedbal** (1874–1930), whose most popular operetta was *Polish Blood*.

Left, above: **The operetta found its way from Paris to Vienna in a very short time. The first successful composer there was Franz von Suppé. This picture is from a production of his operetta** *The Beautiful Galathea.*

Left: **The history of the 'Theater an der Wien' stretches from the time of Mozart and Beethoven right up to performances of modern, light compositions. The picture is from the beginning of the 19th century.**

Above: **From Johann Strauss's operetta** *Die Fledermaus.*

Left: **Johan Strauss's first big success as a composer in the new comedy genre came with the operetta** *Indigo und die vierzig Räuber.* **It was performed for the first time in Vienna in 1871.**

Paris and Vienna are the parents of operetta. Their children, attired according to Parisian or Viennese style, have filled the theatres of all Europe. In Berlin, there was the famous Metropol Theatre (now the Komische Oper, Berlin), with popular composers **Paul Lincke (1866–1946)**, **Jean Gilbert (1879–1942)** and **Eduard Künneke (1885–1935)**, the composer of the still popular *The Cousin from Batavia.*

Operettas were being written and performed in Budapest, Prague and Hamburg. They crossed the Atlantic Ocean and came to anchor in theatres on Broadway. One operetta that won great acclaim there was *Rose Marie* (1916) by the composer **Rudolf Friml (1879–1972)**, a Czech who had settled in the United States. But on the theatrical horizon, a new sun was already rising for a genre that was to shine in the full brightness of the foot-lights and on the silver screen of the coming decade.

The Musical

While New York's Metropolitan Opera House presents the world's opera classics, usually performed in their original language, with world-famous stars and the best conductors, Broadway presents theatregoers with entertaining musicals in the audience's own language. People are usually very interested in shows that present life as it really is in their own country. This is American theatre both in subject and in musical arrangement. Music that is part of a country's culture is always valid, and it was particularly so at the time when this new musical genre was taking shape.

The musical is a descendant of French operetta and English ballad opera. If we investigate its early history, we find minstrel shows, a form of popular entertainment in the United States that dates from the middle of the last century. White actors and singers, their faces blackened, imitated what was supposed to be a black style of singing and way of speaking. They sang songs, danced and performed variety routines.

The musical is also derived from revue, a form of entertainment comprising a variety of sketches without any real continuity of story, which offered the audience a colourful show, full of dancing and music. For a while, the revue dominated both American and European stages, especially in the 1920s. The traditions of the American show and American popular music joined to form the musical.

This did not happen all at once. Transitional forms of musical comedy developed and these gradually crystallized into the classic American musical, as it was later created by Leonard Bernstein.

Among the first of these transitional forms was the American folk *singspiel* of **Jerome Kern** (1885–1945) with *Show Boat*

After an eventful life, Johann Strauss now rests in the Vienna Cemetery.

Franz Lehar is best known for his operetta *The Merry Widow*.

(1927). Its theme was close to the hearts of the American public, as it evoked nostalgic memories of the days when paddle steamers, packed with colourful characters, travelled along the Mississippi River. The song *Ol' Man River*, especially when popularized by Paul Robeson in the film of the show, rightly became an evergreen.

Gershwin's *Porgy and Bess* (1935), a jazz opera with black performers, stands on the borderline between opera and musical. Another important milestone was *Oklahoma* (1943), with music by **Richard Rodgers** (1902–79) and a libretto by Oscar Hammerstein II (1895—1960). Its cowboy theme was, once again, purely American. From the workshop of the same author came an arrangement of Bizet's *Carmen* (1943), as a musical. Its dramatic story appealed to the sentiments of American audiences and the rewarding music succeeded in bridging the gap between the high art of opera and popular theatre.

Among the many rich musical productions of this time, **Irving Berlin** (1888–1989) and his *Annie, Get Your Gun* (1946) and **Cole Porter** (1891–1964) with *Kiss Me, Kate* (1948) are worthy of mention. These were later followed by one of the most successful international musicals of all, *My Fair Lady* (1956), composed by **Frederick Loewe** (1904–88). In it, George Bernard Shaw's play *Pygmalion*

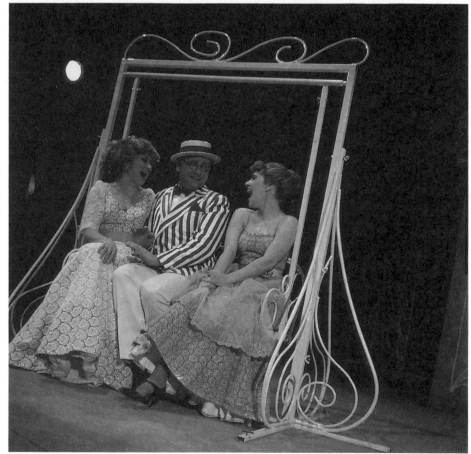

Polish Blood, an operetta by Oskar Nedbal.

The story of Berlin operetta must include the composer Eduard Künneke. His *The Cousin from Batavia* is still being performed.

found new and effective dimensions.

The classic musical is, without doubt, *West Side Story* (1957) by **Leonard Bernstein** (1918–90), based on a libretto by Arthur Laurents with lyrics by Stephen Sondheim. The story is derived from Shakespeare's *Romeo and Juliet*, but transferred from Renaissance Verona to contemporary New York. Instead of the hostile Montagues and Capulets, there are two street gangs, Americans against Puerto Ricans. Their irreconcilable hatred in the face of young love leads to senseless tragedy, in the same way as Shakespeare's drama. The contemporary story was set to music that echoed the development of modern jazz. It was this that made *West Side Story* such a phenomenal success, particularly among young people.

The success of a musical depends not only on its theme, text and music, but also on the casting. Sometimes a musical is written specifically for a particular performer and this ensures the interest of audiences in advance. This was the case with Barbra Streisand, for whom the librettist Isobel Lennart and the composer **Jule Styne** (b. 1905) created *Funny Girl* (1964). The film brought Streisand world acclaim.

The best songs and melodies from musicals circulate around the world on records, tapes, CDs and the radio. If it had not been for Louis Armstrong and his original recording of the central song of the musical *Hello Dolly*, this may never have become a world-wide hit. It is due to him that the song has had such long life.

The rock-opera *Jesus Christ Superstar* by **Andrew Lloyd Webber** had an interesting history. It was first produced as a double album, which in one year, sold two

Leonard Bernstein. Was he more famous for his conducting, his skilful popularization of music, or composing the acclaimed *West Side Story*?

million copies. It was a whole year later that it was staged in New York City. The musical is a continuous sequence of music without any spoken dialogue.

Even before this, a rock band had appeared on the New York scene, taking the place of the traditional theatre orchestra in the musical *Hair*, composed by **Galt MacDermot**. *Hair* was a statement by the younger generation in the United States about their way of life. For example, one of the heroes receives his call-up papers for the Vietnam War and leaves behind his cut-off long hair as a memento for the others members of his gang.

Just as the inspiration for Leonard Bernstein's *West Side Story* was Shakespeare's drama, so the work of England's greatest playwright became the script for the musical *Two Gentleman of Verona*, composed by Galt MacDermot.

Hair, the famous Broadway musical, in Miloš Forman's film adaptation.

Another famous literary source was Cervantes' *Don Quixote*, which was given new life in the musical *Man of La Mancha*, by **Mitch Leigh**.

A measure of success of any show is the number of performances. In American theatres, this sometimes runs to thousands. Some shows run for several years to consistently full houses, amassing great profit for the producers, performers and theatre managers. A few interesting figures include *Hello Dolly*—2,844 performances, *Man of La Mancha*—2,329, *Hair*—1,750 and *Funny Girl*—1,348.

Just as, in their time, records took jazz to Europe, so film adaptations made Europe aware of the American musical. A number of successful musicals are still being staged in Europe and productions of this kind are being carried on by interested artists. One example is the German composer **Franz Grothe** (1908–82) and his musi-

Left: **Gershwin's** *Porgy and Bess* **is a musical dramatic work on the borderline between opera and musical. It has also been filmed.**

Top: **The film version of Bernstein's** *West Side Story.*

Above: **The musical version of Shaw's play** *Pygmalion* **was called** *My Fair Lady.*

87

cal *Das Wirtshaus in Spessart*, based on a successful film.

Every day, there are people waiting to be entertained. Every day, the curtain rises on acting, singing and dancing. Every day librettists and composers sit down at their desks, hoping to provide new works for the stage. It is true now and will be in the future that the most successful will be those telling about the lives of contemporary people, in which contemporary music is played and the dancing is to contemporary taste. Time will determine which musicals will disappear into oblivion and which survive.

Barbra Streisand

Music at Home

We place a compact disc on the CD player and press the button. Our room becomes a concert hall, a cathedral, a theatre, a salon in a castle or in a mansion house. Pressing the button stops time and carries us centuries into the past. Our home can resound to a Berlioz symphony or reverberate to the tremendous ensemble of instruments and voices in a Handel oratorio. Or a Schubert string quartet might fill our home with music that was first played in rooms with more domestic dimensions. We turn down the volume and listen to a conversation between four instruments. This is chamber music, music that was born in homely surroundings. Chamber music grew out of people's natural desire not just to be listeners, but to help create the music too.

Once Upon a Time

The beginnings of 'homemade' music were in the burgher societies of the 16th century. Amateur musicians met in small

Music at home as depicted by Johann Georg Platzer (1704–61). Notice the rich furnishing of the room, the quantity of food and drink and also the musical instruments (from the left): the flute, the lute, the violoncello and the violin.

The colourful array of paintings in one of the salons of the castle at Český Krumlov. It was in just such surroundings that balls and musical performances for home entertainment were held.

groups—a lawyer, a doctor, a professor. In each country they had different names; in Italy *camerata*, in England consorts, in Germany *collegium musicum*. One *collegium musicum* in Frankfurt had a fixed number of nine members (based on the nine Muses), who were allowed to bring three guests at the most (based on the three Graces). All members could sing and each had to play some instrument. They met once a week from five to ten in the evening, sang songs in harmony, discussed music, had supper together and—as a witness revealed—drank in moderation. There was no distinction made between performers and audience.

Music was also cultivated in aristocratic halls and salons. Both host and guests played and sang. Later, with the expansion of instrumental music and the increased requirements of technique, professional musicians were needed. The wealthiest people could afford the upkeep of a full ensemble, others had to manage with just one or two musicians. Musicians became part of the servant class in noble households. They created a pleasant background for banquets, played to evening parties in private parks and serenaded family festivals. During evening concerts the host would boast to his guests about the skill of his musicians. Being in the service of a noble family meant having a guaranteed livelihood and the opportunity to use one's talents. Really influential noblemen had their own maestro, band-leader, and composer all in one person, who had to keep the salon supplied with ever-new scores. Count Eszterhazy had **Joseph Haydn** (1732–1809). At the court of the Prussian King

Joseph Haydn

Above: La Madeleine Church in Paris is a typical example of Neo-Classical architecture from the turn of the 18th century. It was built at the time when Haydn, Mozart and Beethoven were composing.

Frederick II, who was himself an excellent musician and composer, there was a court concert master and composer, **František Benda** (1709–86). Mozart and Beethoven were also dependent on the support of their noble benefactors.

Neo-Classicism

The second half of the 18th century was the golden age of chamber music. At that time, in the works of Haydn, Mozart and Beethoven, the basic types and styles of chamber music were crystallizing. The forms of the classical sonata and cyclical compositions of four movements were becoming stabilized. The most frequently used chamber ensembles came into being: the string quartet, the piano trio, the wind quintet and the duo for solo instrument and piano.

Chamber Music on the Concert Stage

In the 19th century, the regular performance of chamber music was still considered a customary entertainment for the musical amateur. Gradually, however, with the growing demands for

technical agility, chamber music was transferred to the concert stage. The road divided; those who had been performing amateurs became the audience listening to the performance of professional musicians.

Composers

Our musical heritage is immense and is being constantly increased by the compositions of contemporary composers.

The father of the string quartet was **Joseph Haydn**, who wrote 77 of them. Some were given their own names at the time of composition, but most had titles given to

The Eszterhazy Château (now Fertöd, Hungary), where Joseph Haydn was concert master and composer in the service of the aristocratic Eszterhazy family in 1766–90.

A Haydn manuscript—*Divertimento a quattro.*

Franz Schubert was a leading composer of chamber music.

them later as a result of external circumstances or an accidental pronunciation. It is said that when Haydn was once shaving, he declared, 'I'd give my best quartet for a sharp razor.' Hence the *Rasiermesserquartett.*

Beethoven gave an equal role to all four instruments in his string quartets. Earlier, the lead was taken by the first and second violin, and the viola and the violoncello merely formed the accompaniment. Mozart also used wind instruments in chamber music. His best known is the *Clarinet Quintet in A major*, in which the leading voice of the clarinet is added to a string quartet. Mozart dedicated this piece to his friend Anton Stadler, an excellent clarinetist.

Beethoven's sonatas for violin

Ludwig van Beethoven

and piano–*the Kreutzer*, Op. 47 in A major and *Spring (Frühlings-sonate)*, Op. 24 in F major should not be forgotten. He put exceptional emotional and ideological content into his string quartets, and they represent the summit of chamber music, requiring great interpretational abilities. This is particularly true of the last of his 17 compositions for this group of instruments. Beethoven's 'Septet' is also frequently performed. It is a unique chamber work for seven instruments: violin, viola, violoncello, double-bass, clarinet, French horn and bassoon.

Franz Schubert (1797–1828) composed a number of romantic songs, a style that was enjoyed to the full in the salons of the wealthy townsmen of his time. His chamber music was originally also intended for this group. Schubert wrote 20 string quartets, piano and violin sonatas and a quintet with double-bass in which the theme was a variation of the melody of his song 'The Trout' (*Forel-lenquintett*). Similarly, in his string quartet *Death and the Maiden*, he used his song of the same name.

A Czech composer, theoretician and professor at the Paris conservatoire, **Antonín Rejcha** (1770–1836) won acclaim for his compositions for the wind instrument quintet.

Chamber music moved on from its original purpose to become good, popular music of its time, accessible to amateurs and a means of serious expression. In it, we hear the composers confiding to the instruments the sadness and joy of their souls, their experiences and memories. This is true, for instance, of the *String Quartet in E minor No. 1*, 'From my life' by Bedřich Smetana, and also his

Johannes Brahms

Antonín Dvořák

The piano trio is a group of three musicians — a pianist, a violinist and a cellist. *Piano trio* is also the title of the composition played by these three.

The string quartet comprises two violins, a viola and a cello.

Piano Trio in G minor, expressing his sorrow over the loss of a beloved child. The second string quartet of Leoš Janáček, *Intimate Letters*, is a confession of ardent emotion experienced by the septuagenarian composer in the last years of his life.

The works of **Johannes Brahms** (1833–97) have a lasting place on the concert platform. Besides the more usual string quartets and piano trios, Brahms also created compositions in which string and wind instruments are combined, for example a quintet with clarinet and a trio for piano, violin, and French horn.

Antonín Dvořák (1841–1904) is also one of the great masters of chamber music. Among his most inspiring string quartets, are his *Quartet in F major*, Op. 96, called 'The American', and his piano trio 'Dumky', in which the undertones of stylized Slavonic folk music alternate rapidly with melancholic and dance moods. A popular composition is his *Sonatina in G major*, Op. 100 for violin and piano.

From the works of **Tchaikovsky**, there is his *String Quartet in D major*, Op. 11, including the well-known second movement—*Andante cantabile*—in which the melody of a Russian folk song can be heard.

The list of important composers of chamber music can never be complete, but at least a few others must be mentioned. These include **Claude Debussy** (*Sonata for Violin and Piano*), **Maurice Ravel** (1875–1937), Paul Hindemith, Dmitry Shostakovich (1906–75) and Sergey Prokofiev.

The Interpreter

As a general rule, established chamber ensembles take their name from the first violinist or from a composer, such as the Hindemith Quartet and Kolisch Quartet, or from their hometown, country or the composer whose

There was a time when musicians performing in castles wore livery. Now even folk ensembles may give performances there.

work forms the basis of their repertoire, such as the Amadeus Quartet and Smetana Quartet.

A chamber ensemble's interpretation is refined through years of working together. Playing in a professional chamber ensemble means a life-long obligation. Personal and family life become subordinate to the professional work in the ensemble. If one member leaves and has to be replaced, this threatens the standard of the entire ensemble and holds up their development while they repeat their study of the basic repertoire. Some ensembles break up after five or ten years, others continue with changing members and there are those that maintain the same structure for many decades, until the members reach ripe old age.

Right: **Historical instruments displayed in museums call to mind the time of 'homemade' music in the salons of castles and bourgeois homes.**

Below: **The recorder had an important place in Renaissance music in the home.**

Above: **This is not the Pied Piper of Hamelin. It is a schoolmaster and his little band of pipers in a painting by Cyril Bouda.**

The final resting place of Johannes Brahms.

Return of Early Instruments

The instrumental music of the Middle Ages, the Renaissance, and the Early Baroque era has long rested in archives. Over the last few decades, however, it has been brought to the concert stage as an attractive revival. If it is to sound authentic, however, the music should be played on the instruments that were used at the time it was written. Copies of medieval and Renaissance instruments are now being reconstructed, and new, professional ensembles are being formed to play the original music.

As many such compositions do not make huge demands on the skill of the players, this music is gaining popularity among amateurs. The music of past ages is returning to its roots; it is becoming music not only to be listened to, but to give pleasure to the musicians who play it.

Making our own Music

Let us press the button and stop the record-player for a moment. Music is available to us from another source that can be mastered easily without prolonged study. There are very many simple instruments that were thought up for children by the composer Carl Orff, and with which one can pass pleasant moments without much learning. For example, there is the recorder which is exceptionally suitable for making music at home. If a music teacher who is fond of children can be found, then the children will readily follow him on her into the world of music, as they did the Pied Piper of Hamelin.

Music for Concert Halls

We can listen to orchestral concerts at home in comfort by simply switching on the radio, record-player, tape recorder, television or video. Despite this, thousands of people take the trouble to go to concert halls. They want to be where it happens; they want not only to hear but also to see with their own eyes—not at one remove—how music is made, how the musicians interpret it, how they bring the composer's score alive. They want to have the live experience of music, and they want to enjoy it in the company of others.

Below: **The message from the composers is conveyed from the stage.**

Above: **A concert hall is something like a cathedral, where we can experience the exultant moment of an encounter with art.**

Although concerts are a daily occurrence in large cities, each one is something of a gala occasion, both for the audience and for the musicians. This is apparent from the way the musicians are dressed and how they behave; there is a kind of ritual about it that has stabilized over the centuries and is traditionally maintained by orchestras all over the world.

Let us see what happens before each concert and who the people are who help to prepare it.

What shall we Play?

The principal conductor and the director of the orchestra plan the programme for the concert season a long time in advance. They know the repertoire, they study the scores and decide whether this or that piece of music is suitable for performance. They consider which compositions should be played on the same evening and in what order. They go to concerts given by other orchestras and travel to festivals abroad to get an idea of what is being played generally and to obtain new modern pieces for their orchestra. They also choose conductors and soloists whom they wish to invite for guest performances.

In some orchestras, this task is entrusted to a particular person, the musical adviser. He or she must have a comprehensive education in music, they are usually musicologists, and must have a detailed knowledge of the history of music as well as an awareness of modern developments. The adviser provides the public with information on planned concerts and also obtains information about the compositions for the printed programmes.

There is plenty to chose from—thousands of symphonies, symphonic poems, suites, overtures, concertos for solo instruments with orchestra, cantatas and oratorios. The works of the important composers of the past are listed in

Herbert von Karajan is conducting. What can the musicians read from his expression?

thematic catalogues, where information is supplied on all their compositions. The tremendous number of works by Bach, Mozart and Schubert is astonishing—which just shows how very diligent the old masters were.

Nevertheless, when assessing

the importance of a composer, we must not be misled by the quantity of his works. The number of symphonies says nothing about the quality of the works. Let us take a look at some interesting comparisons.

Beethoven composed nine sym-

Bedřich Smetana, the composer of *My Country*, a cycle of symphonic poems.

Left: In the beginning is an idea: a flash of inspiration, a compulsion. That is how Antonín Dvořák described the first bars of his *New World Symphony*.

98

phonies; so, too, did Dvořák; Tchaikovsky wrote six symphonies, Brahms four, Martinů six, Mozart forty-nine, and if Joseph Haydn were alive today, he would stand a chance of getting into the *Guinness Book of Records* as the composer of 104 symphonies!

Sometimes a composer gives a piece a special title, which hints at the content or his non-musical inspiration. So, for instance, Beethoven called his third symphony *Eroica* ('Heroic') and his sixth symphony *Pastoral*. The naming of his fifth symphony *Fateful* did not originate with him. Mendelssohn wrote *Italian* and *Scottish* symphonies, while Dvořák has *From the New World*.

Quite frequently, however, a composition is not named by the composer but according to an external event, perhaps the place where it was first performed. Dvořák's eighth symphony in G major is called the *English*, because the score was published in London and it was performed in Cambridge, with Dvořák conducting. Mozart wrote symphonies

A page of an orchestral score. The conductor has marked changes in the beat, the entry of some instruments and the tempo.

called *Linz, Parisian, Prague, Haffner* and *Jupiter*. We find a mixed palette of symphonies by Joseph Haydn; for instance, the *Surprise* symphony, so called because of the sudden surprise of the timpano in the second movement and the *Clock, Farewell, Bear, Imperial, Hen, Maria Theresa, Schoolmaster, Roxolane* and *Laudon*.

It is usually important to know in advance how long a composition takes to play, especially if the concert is to be broadcast live. Modern composers usually give this information on the score, using the Italian word *durata*, or duration, and to some extent this also decides the tempo of the work for the players. This was not the

Chronologisch-thematisches Verzeichnis
sämtlicher Tonwerke

Wolfgang Amade Mozarts

nebst Angabe der verlorengegangenen, angefangenen,
übertragenen, zweifelhaften und unterschobenen Kompositionen

von Dr. Ludwig Ritter von Köchel

Nachdruck der dritten,
von Alfred Einstein bearbeiteten Auflage

VEB BREITKOPF & HÄRTEL MUSIKVERLAG

Köchel's list of Mozart's works. For instance, on page 668 we find the start of the opera *Don Giovanni*.

opus ('work') to name them. When important composers did not do this or did not number all their works, the job is taken on by musicologists, who make detailed catalogues of the composer's works. The compositions are then marked with their number in the catalogue. For example, Mozart's catalogue was compiled by Ludwig von Köchel; Haydn's works were catalogued by Anthony van Hoboken. (*Verzeichnis* means 'index'.) For example:

J. S. Bach, *Passion According to St. Matthew*
 BMV (Bach-Werke-Verzeichnis) 244

G. F. Handel, *Messiah*
 HWV (Handel-Werke-Verzeichnis) 56

J. Haydn, *Symphony in G major, Op. 94*
 Hob (Anthony van Hoboken) I/94

W. A. Mozart, *Eine Kleine Nachtmusik*
 KV (Köchel-Verzeichnis) 525

case in the past, when the tempo of a piece was left to the conductor to decide.

A comparison between recordings of the length of performance of several compositions, interpreted by different orchestras and conductors, is interesting.

Beethoven, *Ninth symphony in D minor*
 Berliner Philharmoniker, cond.
 H. v. Karajan   65 min. 15 sec.
 Gewandhaus-Orchester Leipzig, cond. F. Konwitschny
          71 min. 40 sec.

Smetana, *Vltava*
 Czech Philharmonic, cond.
 V. Talich   12 min. 10 sec.

 NBC Symphony Orchestra, cond.
 A. Toscanini   10 min. 55 sec.
 Berliner Philharmoniker, cond.
 H. v. Karajan   10 min.

Ravel, *Bolero*
 Orchestra Lamoureux, cond. M. Ravel   17 min. 15 sec.
 Boston Symphony Orchestra, cond. S. Koussevitski
          14 min. 34 sec.
 Philadelphia Orchestra, cond. E. Ormandy   15 min.
 Berliner Philharmoniker, cond.
 H. v. Karajan   12 min.

The Organization of Works

Most composers number their compositions using the Latin word

The Conductor

The short time that the conductor is on the concert stage is a small part of his or her working life. The main part of the conductor's activity lies in preparatory work at home and in rehearsals.

First of all, he studies the score. He reads the parts of all the instruments and their combinations to obtain an idea of the overall sound and the course of the composition. Some conductors play the score on the piano (one of a conductor's essential skills). Others prefer silent reading; they have cultivated a perfect image of orchestral sound and from the score alone can imagine how the whole composition will sound.

The conductor plans the time divisions of the work and decides its tempo and dynamic flow. He decides which group of instruments and which solo instruments should be enhanced, and which, at a given moment, softened. He will mark the score with a pencil in the places where he needs to make a clear gesture to alert a player to come in or to change the tempo and so on.

When a composition is new to the orchestra, the conductor usually limits the information he passes on to the players to a brief description of the content of the composition. After this, he conveys his conception mainly by gestures. These are the result of long years of tradition and are known to players the world over. The conductor 'plays' the orchestra as he would play a musical instrument.

There are very few conductors who give any thought to what the audience might think of their gestures and behaviour. A conductor's concern is concentrated on the most effective way of expressing his conception of the music through gestures that will be understood by the players. A few

How conductors used to perform: Lully marked the beat by striking the ground with a long walking stick. Mozart conducted the orchestra from the harpsichord, as did his contemporaries. Weber held a roll of paper in his hand to emphasize his hand movements. Later, though, the baton, the magic wand and powerful instrument of all conductors, came into general use.

Diagram of the basic conducting movements. The hand of the conductor 'sketches' a figure in the air which determines the beat: double time, triple time, quadruple time, six-beat time.

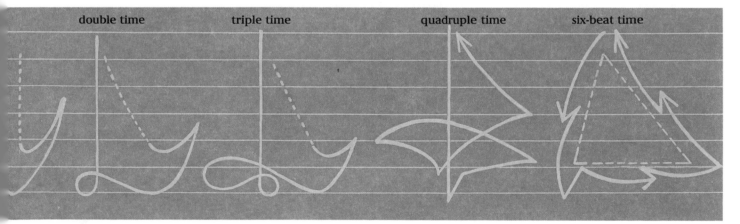

double time   triple time   quadruple time   six-beat time

The orchestra is governed by Leonard Bernstein.

Václav Neumann conducting.

conductors—they are mainly in the pop music business—make a point of cultivating external effects and because of this, they are called 'show-conductors'. It is said that they practise their performance in front of a mirror. If asked about this, though, it is not likely that they would admit it!

The Conductor's 'Instrument'

The symbol of the modern conductor is his baton. This has not always been the case. In the 18th century, the orchestra was usually led by the first violinist, the concert-master from his stand, or the harpsichord player via the band-master. The use of the baton is attributed to J. B. Lully, court musician-in-chief to the French King Louis XIV, who marked the beat by banging a heavy walking-stick. From this originated the French expression for 'marking the beat', *battre la mesure.* It proved fatal for Lully; he once struck his foot with the stick, the wound festered and he died from the injury.

Mozart directed the orchestra, even in the theatre, from the harpsichord. Later, conductors held a roll of paper to make the movement of their hands more visible. It was only at the beginning of the 19th century that the conductor's baton gradually came into use. The baton with which Wagner, Liszt, Bülow, Smetana and Dvořák conducted was usually a short decorated stick, often very heavy and sometimes with an ornamental lyre on its end. The modern baton is a slim stick, as light as possible, with a thickened end to rest comfortably in the palm. However, the baton is just an aid; the 'instrument' of the conductor is really the entire orchestra.

Each performance is not only an exceptional mental strain for the conductor, but also demands a physical output similar to that of an athlete. It has been reckoned that during a single evening, the conductor of a symphony orchestra loses three to four kilograms (seven to eight pounds).

Can an orchestra play without a conductor? A small orchestra, like those that played in the time of Haydn or Mozart, could and may do so even today. Even then, one of the players, usually the concert-master, must supervise the rehearsals, determine the manner of interpretation and, during the performance, guide the course of the composition with an inconspicuous nod of the head or motion of his bow. A large symphony orchestra, with about 100 players, especially if it is joined by a choir and soloists, cannot get by without a conductor. Players seated on opposite sides of the stage do not hear each other, and without the intervention of the conductor, such a large group would not be able to maintain precise coordination. Quite apart from this, 100 people would hardly agree on the tempo, the dynamics or the flow of the composition. It is only the conductor who can decide all of this.

Let us look at some prominent

Left: A rather unusual shot—an interval in an orchestral rehearsal. The musicians are having a rest and the conductor is studying the score.

Below: A symphony orchestra in the radio studio. This is a rehearsal not yet using the microphone.

A specimen of an orchestral score for the harp. The players are making notes in the score about the position of pedals. Three are for the left foot (d, c, h) and four for the right (e, f, g, a).

conductors of both the past and the present. It used to be the custom for compositions to be directed for the first time by their composers. Remember that, in the 18th century, many composers were also band or concert-masters of the ensembles of the gentry, and it was their duty to introduce their own works. Beethoven, too, sometimes conducted his own compositions and we would probably be surprised at his unusual way of doing so. He would indicate *pianissimo* ('very softly') by bending his knees and during dynamic parts, he would jump into the air. Liszt, Wagner, Berlioz, Smetana, Dvořák and Mahler were all conductors. In the present century, with a few exceptions, the professions of composing and conducting have been separated.

Some of the masters of the baton achieved world popularity and became legendary figures.

The usual arrangement of the players in a symphony orchestra.

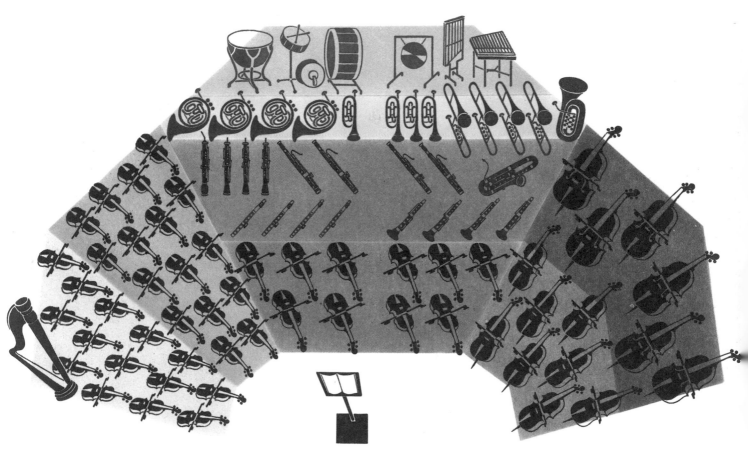

One such was the Italian **Arturo Toscanini** (1867–1957), one of the greatest conductors in the world, famous for his work with the La Scala, Milan, and the New York Metropolitan Opera House. For many years, he also conducted the world-famous NBC (National Broadcasting Company) Symphony Orchestra. A star of the first magnitude was the American conductor of Polish origin, **Leopold Stokowski** (1882–1977). Another name that has become a legend is that of **Herbert von Karajan** (1908—89), for many years principal of the Wiener Philharmoniker and the Berliner Philharmoniker, and also artistic director of the Viennese Staatsoper and the Salzburger Festspiele. Ranked with these is the famous American Leonard Bernstein, who was both conductor and composer and an exception to the rule of two separate professions.

The names of some conductors are linked inseparably with particular orchestras, whose high standards are credited to them. A few examples are **Václav Talich** (1883–1961) of the Czech Philharmonic, **Willem Mengelberg** (1871–1951) and the Concertgebouw-Orkest Amsterdam, **Serge Koussevitski** (1874–1951) and the Boston Symphony Orchestra, and **Evgeny Mravinsky** (1903–88) and the Leningrad Philharmonic.

The Members of the Orchestra

Whatever are they doing all day if they only come along in the evening to play for two hours? A closer look at the activities of the members of an orchestra reveals that the burden of their work and responsibility is no less than that of doctors, teachers, pilots or any

The orchestra is joined by a mixed choir to perform a cantata or oratorio.

other professional who takes his work seriously. They must all have an extensive professional education to university level. Among them will be outstanding virtuosos who voluntarily give up their artistic individuality to place their skills at the service of the whole, and who become submissive to the will of the conductor. They practise at home, maintain their technical dexterity and study the more difficult passages of their parts well in advance.

The main part of an orchestra player's work is at rehearsals. These involve hours of concentration, when each member adapts himself to the teamwork of the group. He watches every movement of the conductor and must not let his attention stray for

a single moment, even when the composer assigns to him a long 'tacet', or silence. He then silently counts the empty beats so that he comes in on time with his own solo.

For a single evening concert, the orchestra usually has three to four rehearsals, each lasting four to five hours. Once the concert is over, rehearsals start again the next day for the next programme. If the orchestra is planning a tour, especially a tour abroad, it must study the whole programme in advance. There is usually no opportunity during a tour for regular rehearsing. A lot of time is taken up travelling, frequently every day and even at night — flights and journeys from place to place and from hotel to hotel. Be-

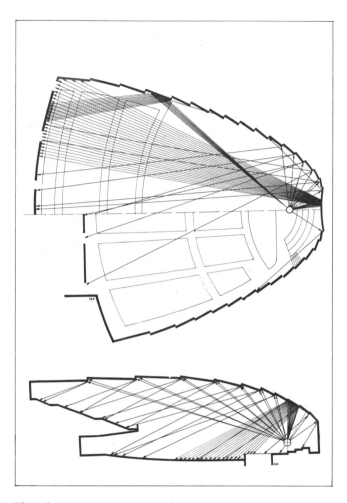

The plan (ground plan and lateral cross-section) shows the acoustic solution of a modern concert hall. The walls and ceiling are profiled in broken lines to deflect the sound waves back to the auditorium and to ensure that the whole space is filled in a balanced manner with the sound coming from the stage (marked by a circle in its ideal centre).

fore a concert, there is a short acoustical, or 'seating' rehearsal, so that each member knows his place on the stage, and so that the conductor becomes familiar with the acoustics of the hall. If the concert is to be recorded or transmitted, the sound director attends this rehearsal so that he can hear the sound of the orchestra and position his microphones.

The Keeper of the Records

He lives concealed among shelves full of musical scores and sheets. Audiences are never aware of his existence. He takes care of the treasures that have accumulated during the years of the orchestra's life. Sometimes, there are precious relics among the archives, such as scores that have been handwritten by the composer. Many musical scores carry notes made decades earlier by a famous conductor when he used them in his work.

The keeper of the records has the task of preparing sheet music for the entire orchestra. Long before rehearsals start, the conductor is given the score. When the concert is to be recorded or broadcast, the music director must also receive a score. Not all the compositions played by an orchestra at the concerts are stored in its records. Sometimes the music must be borrowed from another orchestra or an agency—sometimes even from another country.

Just as a point of interest, the score of Dvořák's *Symphony in E minor* (the 'New World') has 204 pages. Printed sheets for the entire orchestra amount to about 700 sheets and weigh 5 kilograms (11 pounds).

The Orchestra

The seating of a symphony orchestra on the stage is always the same. The first violin sits to the left of the conductor; further on, from left to right, the other string instruments; the wind, brass and reed instruments sit in the back rows; and the percussion group is right at the back. Some conductors require slight changes, but in general this pattern is maintained.

A modern symphony orchestra has 100 to 120 members. The modern orchestra developed during the 19th century; earlier orchestras, however, were much smaller. For instance, the orchestra of the Prussian King Frederick II had only 10 members; Haydn's orchestra at the residence of Count Eszterhazy numbered 24 musicians. At the première of Handel's oratorio *Messiah,* there were 33 members of the orchestra, but when it was played in 1859 at a gala concert held in London's Crystal Palace to mark the centenary of Handel's death, the performers numbered around 4,000 musicians and singers. Hector Berlioz required a gigantic orchestra for the performance of his *Requiem.* The instruments included 18 double basses, 12 French horns and 16 timpani. Gustav Mahler's Eighth symphony, the *Symphony of Thousands,* calls for a full symphony orchestra with the addition of a number of other instruments, several harps, campanelle, celesta, an organ and a harmonium. There are also eight solo singers, a children's choir and two mixed choirs; altogether, nearly 1,000 performers.

Before the orchestra appears, the stage is invaded by a team of stage-hands who set out the chairs, the music-stands and the instruments. Finally, they distribute the sheet music for each player. Some knowledge of music is needed for this, too, to make sure the right part is put on the right music-stand. When an orchestra is going on tour, the first to set out are trucks carrying the instruments. This is because harps, timpani, double-basses, violoncello, tubas and trombones cannot be transported in coaches or in the cabins of planes. They also carry chests full of music and scores, and others containing tail coats.

The Concert Hall

When the arts ceased to be the exclusive property of the aristocracy, institutions were set up to arrange public concerts, with entrance fees for town audiences. Suitable rooms for concerts were found in inns, former monasteries and theatres. For example, the Leipzig Gewandhaus-Orchestra got its name from the place where it first performed; from 1781 it gave concerts on the premises of a Leipzig drapers, in a hall big enough to hold 500 people.

Modern concert halls are built to hold 2,000 to 3,000 people. Everyone wants to hear well, even in the back seats. All the groups of instruments in the orchestra must sound well-balanced, the sound of the choir should blend well with the orchestra and the voices of soloists must not be lost. The whole range of music must be audible, from the low frequency of the tuba and double bass to the highest notes of the piccolo. All of this depends on the shape and size of the hall and the covering of the walls and ceiling. This is why one of the skills of an architect, especially one involved in designing public places, is to master the properties of special acoustics.

Sound spreads in all directions from its source. In a concert hall, it is partially swallowed up by the walls, the ceiling, the upholstery

Left, above: **The Royal Albert Hall in London (1871) holds an audience of 10,000.**

Left: **Rafael Kubelík, one of the leading conductors of the present day.**

107

Music played at royal occasions on the Thames in the time of Handel. The picture is the work of an Italian artist, Giovanni Antonio Canal, called Canaletto (1697–1768).

a special event, not just because of the importance of the music, but also because of the setting.

Nowadays, a concert lasts about two hours at most. In the past, it lasted much longer and the programme was much more varied: solo pieces alternated with orchestral pieces, the instrumentalist performed as conductor and also as soloist. He also had to show a knowledge of improvisation; sometimes someone in the audience simply would give him a theme to play to. When public concerts began, they often lasted several hours, perhaps from five in the afternoon until eleven in the evening. Refreshments were served and quite often the audience disturbed the players with their conversation. Even in the middle of the 19th century, gala concerts started at midday.

of the seats and the clothing of the audience. High frequencies spread in a straight line and are absorbed to a greater degree than low ones. Each hall has a specific reverberation time. This means that at the moment when the source of the sound dies down, the sound lingers for a period of time up to several seconds. When the hall is full, this time is shorter; when it is empty, the time is longer. With lower frequencies, the reverberation is longer, with higher tones it is shorter because high tones die away earlier, deep tones resound for longer. The architect must, therefore, take these facts into account. He must determine correctly the shape and size of the hall, the surface and angle of its walls and the type of floor covering. Some materials, such as textiles, porous materials and leather, deaden sound, others like smooth plaster, marble and glass repel it.

Let us compare some statistics on acoustics of a couple of concert halls.

The new Gewandhaus, Leipzig: length 54 metres (182 feet), width 42 metres (142 feet), median height 16 metres (54 feet); seating 1,905 people; total volume 21.650 cubic metres (73 cubic feet), that is, 11.3 cubic metres (38 cubic feet) per member of the audience; the stage has an area of 183 cubic metres (617 cubic feet); the reverberation time in the empty hall is 2.2 seconds and in a full hall 2 seconds.

The House of Artists in Prague has a reverberation time of 2.5 seconds, the Royal Festival Hall in London 1.5 seconds, and the Festspielhaus in Bayreuth is the same.

The Audience

A symphony concert is, in its way,

Untraditional Concerts

Sometimes we are able to listen to music somewhere other than in the concert hall, for example in parks, in the gardens of mansion houses and in open-air theatres. The acoustics of such environments are not always ideal, because music in the open air disappears without reverberation. Even so, such concerts have charm.

There was a time when music was written for just such occasions. For example, Handel's *Water Music* was played to the royal family as it took a trip on the Thames and his *Music for the Royal Fireworks* was performed in London's Green Park in 1749, when an unusually large number of musicians took part — about seventy.

The Cheapest Instrument

It is not for sale, you cannot buy it with money; we receive it when we are born. The instrument—our voice—is something we carry with us all the time. It is our mark of identification, part of our individuality.

The Mystery of the Voice

In a diagram in a textbook of anatomy, the voice looks very simple. A description of how the human voice works can also be easily understood.

A stream of air from the lungs passes through a gap between two tiny muscles, the vocal chords. These vibrate in the same way as, for example, the double reed of the oboe or the bassoon. Depending on how much they are stretched, they produce a high or low tone. This is only the basic tone; if it were isolated from the surrounding muscles and cavities, or if it were produced with artificial vocal chords, it would be nothing at all like a human voice. It would be very feeble and its

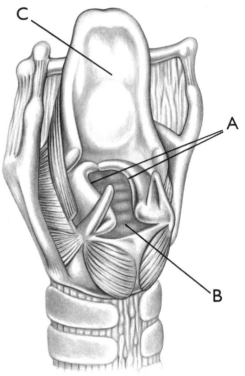

Above: **The voice box is situated in the throat: (A) the vocal chords (plicae vocales), (B) the glottis (rima glottidis), (C) the epiglottis.**

Left: **The acoustics of the interior of a church magnify the impression gained from the powerful harmony of human voices.**

timbre or individual overtones probably would sound like a partyblower.

The strength of the tone produced is determined by the shape of the chords that we are born with, and by the strength of exhaling air, which we can control. The timbre of a voice is determined by the resounding cavities in the chest and the head, the construction of the body, the muscles and the bones. This is similar to the

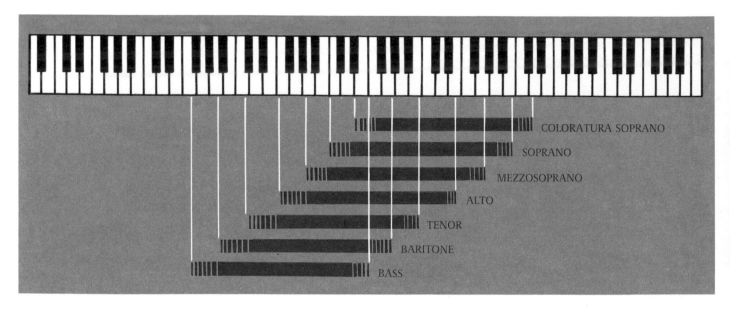

The voices of singers have various tone ranger.

strings of a violin: the true sound of a violin depends on the re-sounding space of the wooden corpus or sound box.

The human body is not mass produced. You cannot find two people in the world who are exactly the same down to the smallest detail. Detectives identify a culprit by his fingerprints. We recognize our friends by their voices and we can recognize an actor or a singer from a recording. Each voice is as individual and unique as its owner.

Among the basic features of a voice are its strength and its timbre. In addition, there is the way the voice is used, the individual inflection of vowels and consonants, pronunciation and speed of speech. There are also differences in the way members of different ethnic groups use their voices.

Together with our lips and tongues, our voices serve us as a means of explanation, for conveying emotion, and for artistic expression. A folk singer has no problem in the technique of singing; he sings in the style that he has inherited from his forebears and from what he hears around him. However, if a voice is to serve as a means for more exacting artistic expression, then specialized training over a long time, sometimes a number of years, is required. Many operatic and concert singers still visit their teachers, even after they have become professionals, in order to maintain and develop the capability of their voices.

When learning to play an instrument, every beginner proceeds in a similar manner, but there is no such recipe for learning to sing. Each voice is different and each requires a different approach. This is where the best singing teachers demonstrate their skill. Mastering technique is only the first step in learning the art of singing.

'Canto Ergo Sum'

'I sing, therefore I am.' This is a variation of the famous statement by the philosopher René Descartes—*Cogito ergo sum* ('I think, therefore I am') and was coined by the Czech composer **Jaroslav Křička (1882–1969)**, who devoted a large part of his work to vocal music as his artistic creed. He added, 'Singing is proof of my existence.'

Folk Songs

For our ancestors, singing was

The folk song. A mother's lullaby was always the first song a new-born child heard in its cradle.

The songs of wandering minstrels used to bring 'the latest news'. From such a song we learn of the destructive earthquake which struck Lisbon in 1755.

a natural form of expression. They voiced their feelings about all kinds of situations in life in song. They would sing while working, when enjoying themselves, at weddings and to lull a child to sleep. They sang in church and in the pub. Lovesick young men and girls gave expression to their longings in song and soldiers on the march sang to overcome tiredness and to keep in step. Songs by unknown composers spread from village to village by oral tradition and were enriched by new variations of the words and the tunes. No one sang from written notes, for there was no one to write them; there were no lyricists or composers. Songs usually arose from the mood of the moment, the words and the tune coming

into existence together. There was usually no difference between the singer and those who listened to him—every one was singing for pleasure.

Every nation has its own treasure-chest of songs. These would have disappeared long ago if specialists had not set out in search of folk singers and recorded

Franz Schubert

The musical society around Franz Schubert. (Reproduction of a painting by Moritz von Schwind from 1868.)

in their notebooks songs that, until then, had only been preserved in the memory of generations. Printed collections of folk songs and folk poems moved from the village to the town to become a welcome addition to urban social life. Their melodies even influenced the composition of classical music. Composers used, rewrote and incorporated them to express their national identity and the national character of their music. Typical examples are Glinka, Smetana, Grieg, Janáček and Bartók. **Gustav Mahler** (1860–1911) was inspired by German folk poems when he composed the texts for his well-known collection *Des Kaben Wunderhorn* ('Youth's Magic Horn'), which was published at the beginning of the century by Achim von Arnim and Clemens Brentano.

At the turn of the 19th and 20th centuries, recording technology came to the assistance of collectors. One of the first to use it was the Hungarian composer **Béla Bartók** (1881–1945) who made about 8,000 recordings of Hungarian, Slovak and Romanian folk music on a primitive phonograph.

The Art Song

'Night and the Dark.' A rider carrying a child in his arms hurries through the night. The little boy is in a feverish delirium. Out of the fog he sees mysterious beings emerge—the king of the spirits and his daughters—as if they wanted to seize him. The boy dies in terror at the idea that he is to become the prey of the evil spirits.

Franz Schubert wrote his famous song 'King of the Spirits' when he was 18 years old, at the same time that Weber was working on his opera *Der Freischütz*.

A romantic landscape from the beginning of the 19th century could form the setting for songs by Schubert.

Schubert marked it as his first opus. With this song he showed that he was already a true master of the romantic song.

The background to this ballad-like story is a dark stormy night. If we recall the midnight scene from Weber's *Der Freischütz* we see that the two scenes have something in common. They capture the Romanticism of young town society and its liking of mysterious fairy-tale themes.

During his short life, Schubert wrote more than 600 songs. He set to music the poetry of his contemporaries, whose subjects were in harmony with the interests of their generation: romantic rambles through the countryside with its mountain streams, valleys and clacking mills; gazing at the simple beauty of a wild rose or a trout in crystal-clear water. Along with mysterious scenery, these are the things that interested young people and lured them out of the towns into the countryside on foot, with a bundle over their shoulders.

Schubert wrote complicated piano parts for his songs. They are not just accompaniments, but combine with the singing as an equally important aspect of the interpretation of the song's poetic content. Schubert's songs were sung in home surroundings and in the salons of town-houses, where musicians and writers used to meet in a relaxed atmosphere to make music, read verses and discuss the arts and the times. His songs became the popular music of that era.

Composing chamber songs started with Schubert and was developed by Robert Schumann, Hugo Wolf (1860–1903), Johannes Brahms, Richard Strauss and Gustav Mahler. By then, this type of composition was gradually emerging from private salons and mounting the steps to the public concert stage.

The Miracle of the Microphone

The large concert hall requires a singer with a powerful voice. Even now, when electro-acoustics are well developed, the concert singer and, of course, the operatic performer must manage without a microphone. On the other hand, electrical amplifiers are taken for granted in pop music, allowing a voice that is weak to equal the noisest of bands.

What the Voice Can Do

Instrumental music can also be reproduced by the voice. The

An essential accessory of a pop singer is the microphone.

skilled production of tone, the mobility of the voice and precise intonation (tuning) make it possible to convey the transcription of an instrumental composition. Specialized groups of singers, on the border-line betwen classical and pop music, perform instrumental works, such as those of Bach, Mozart and Haydn, arranged for the singing sextet, supplemented with a modern rhythmic group. The power of the voice is not decisive; the necessary intensity and dynamic balancing of the group is achieved with microphones and a sound-master.

The Art of Choral Singing

Choral singing has existed in Europe for several centuries. The broad stream of vocal music for the concert stage gradually separrated from sung liturgy and continued to develop parallel to instrumental music. Large choirs became a counterpart to important symphonic orchestras. Typical works include the oratorios of

The huge choral stadium in Tallin, Estonia, is the scene of regular song festivals in which thousands of singers participate.

Handel, Haydn, Berlioz and Dvořák, sung by choirs numbering several hundred, or even thousands of singers. England, especially, has a rich tradition of choral singing founded on the works of Handel.

In some countries, choral singing by amateurs mainly developed in the last century, when people came together to create singing associations. This not only offered a means of social enjoyment but also strengthened national awareness. Compositions for choirs, uncomplicated and intended for amateur singers at first, developed in complexity, with composers making use of the modern means of expression of contemporary music.

Song and choral festivals now have their own significance, not only as an opportunity to present important choral works to large audiences, but also because they are a chance for amateurs to enjoy a shared experience and to express their common ideas. They are held in a number of European countries. In Latvia, Estonia and Lithuania, choirs numbering many thousands of singers gather at special choral stadiums for nationwide song festivals.

The Children Sing

In the world of music, children's choirs occupy their own special territory. They range from singing simple uncomplicated songs to the interpretation of serious compositions for choirs. In the past,

Bambini di Praga, a well-known children's choir.

More than 200 participants are guided by the baton of the conductor when performing an oratorio. On the stage are soloists, children's, female and male voice choirs and a large symphony orchestra.

monasteries and large churches had choirs made up of young boys and there are still many famous choristers' schools today. The boys lived in the monasteries and were trained for a future as church singers and instrumentalists. Boy sopranos and contraltos raised their voices in pleasing harmony with the choir of mature male voices.

Most children's choirs are now mixed. Often the girls' voices stand out because when a boy's voice breaks, he usually leaves the choir. Choirs sing with symphony orchestras, in theatres and on the radio. Older children's choirs have been a source of inspiration to modern composers, who have written specially for them. In such compositions, choral and solo singing is often combined with elements of drama. In Germany **Paul Hindemith** wrote for children's voices; for example, the children's opera *We Are Building a Town*. In Hungary **Zoltán Kodály** (1882–1967) wrote for children and in England, **Benjamin Britten** composed *A Ceremony of Carols, Noye's Fludde* and an opera, *The Little Sweep*, featuring children.

Everything Makes a Sound

Bells, Little Bells and Percussion Instruments

At midday, on holy days, bells resound over the town. Their sound is exactly as it was several centuries ago. While ancient musical instruments have long been silent, bells are reliable witnesses to the sounds of their times.

Is a bell a musical instrument? It might seem to have no place in this book, but its metal surface reverberates when struck in the same way as the drum, the xylophone and the triangle. Its basic tone is fixed precisely. It can be detected by ear, although at the same time it produces a whole spectrum of harmonic tones that give it its characteristic sound colour. The bell's basic tone, as well as all its harmonious components, is decided by the calculations and sketches on the bell-founder's desk. Once the bell has been cast, its voice cannot be changed; a bell cannot be retuned.

When several bells of different sizes are placed in a bell tower, their basic tones must be set at strictly defined intervals. These models of harmony are determined by tradition and adhered to by bell-founders to this day. Bells, little bells and tiny bells. The smaller the bell, the higher the tone it gives; the bigger, the deeper and more powerful its tone and the more it carries over long distances. A carillon is made up of bells of varying sizes. They are sounded either automatically or with the help of a keyboard. The sounds that ring out from a bell tower may be folk songs or the works of composers. Every hour, bells in Salzburg chime out melodies from the operas of Mozart. In Helsinki, you can hear compositions by **Jean Sibelius** (1865–1957). The Netherlands can boast of the largest number of these beautiful instruments, having about 160, five of them in Amsterdam.

How Sound is Made

When we toss a stone into the middle of a pond, the surface is disturbed and the waves spread outwards in concentric circles, gradually becoming weaker and weaker until they disappear. When we strike a tuned metal object with a hammer—a bell, a gong, the bar of a xylophone or the strings of a piano or harpsichord—or when we pluck the strings of a guitar or a harp or harpsichord, the air is disturbed in regular vibrations. The sound wave spreads in all directions and

Right, above: **In some countries bells are hung inside towers. In southern Europe they are usually placed in open campaniles.**

Right: **The carillon on the tower of the Salzburg palace plays the Papageno aria from Mozart's** *Magic Flute.*

The largest bell in the world is a tourist attraction in the courtyard of the Kremlin in Moscow. It is over 6 metres high (19 ½ feet) and weighs 200 tons. But it has never sounded. It cracked in a fire before it could be placed in a bell tower.

reaches our ears at a speed of about 330 metres (1,110 feet) per second. The tone created by the striking of the hammer weakens until it disappears completely.

If a flexible object vibrates 440 times per second, we hear an A in the middle of the treble clef. It has a frequency of the 440 hertz (hertz is a unit of frequency equal to one cycle per second). When the vibration is doubled to 880 hertz, the tone sounds higher by one octave, and when the vibration is halved, the tone is one octave lower.

Objects that Can be Played

Metal, wood, stretched skin, glass, porcelain—musical instruments can be constructed from all of these. Drinking glasses of different sizes can be played and with a wooden hammer one can play a xylophone, a marimba and the metal bars of a vibraphone. People have discovered a huge number of other objects that can be played, although the precise tone cannot be determined, such as drums, cymbals, castanets and the triangle.

The tone range of musical instruments.

1 Piccolo
2 Flute
3 Oboe
4 Cor anglais (English Horn)
5 Clarinet B flat
6 Saxophone E flat
7 Bassoon

8 French horn
9 Trumpet
10 Trombone
11 Tuba

12 Percussion

13 Violin
14 Viola
15 Violoncello
16 Double bass

17 Guitar
18 Harp
19 Piano

20 Organ

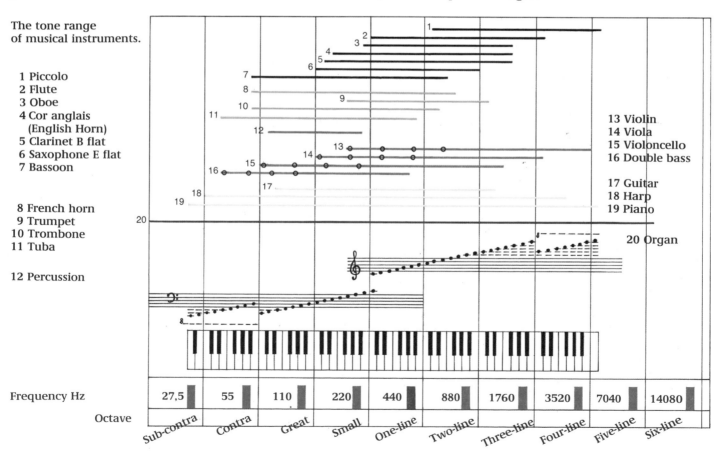

Frequency Hz	27,5	55	110	220	440	880	1760	3520	7040	14080
Octave	Sub-contra	Contra	Great	Small	One-line	Two-line	Three-line	Four-line	Five-line	Six-line

Such instruments, known as the percussion group, support the rhythmic aspect of music. They also sometimes assert themselves, even at the expense of the other parts of musical expression. A dance band cannot exist without percussion instruments and they are taking on an increasingly important role in symphonic music. At the time of classicism, an orchestra got by with a pair of timpani in two different tones that emphasized the rhythm and supported the basic tones of the harmony. Today, separate solo and chamber pieces are written for percussion instruments and their players reach the same level of proficiency as their colleagues playing classical instruments.

As yet, there is no one in the list of virtuoso, percussionists to compare with, say, Franz Liszt, **Niccolò Paganini** (1782–1840) or **Pablo Casals** (1876–1973), the famous Spanish cellist. That is unless we count among them the legendary companologist, or bell ringer, Quasimodo, whose purpose in life became the ringing of the bells in the Notre Dame cathedral in Paris, for whom Victor Hugo erected a lasting monument in his novel.

Singing Wood

In a certain little town they were once repairing the church and in doing so, changed the beams that supported the choir gallery. A violin-maker heard about this and wasted no time buying up the church's old beams. He sawed them up into planks and for years afterwards built excellent violins from them. A poet would, perhaps, say that such old wood, which had rested for several centuries, was 'soaked' with the music of the organ and the church singing and that was why the violins had such a splendid sound. However, the violin-maker thought along much more practical lines; the wood was regular in growth, it was mature, perfectly dried and had a suitable structure.

The work of every violin-maker starts with the selection of the wood. He needs pine for the table of the violin and sycamore for the back. The violin-maker uses his

Left, above: **A set of percussion instruments for a dance band—a reliable 'supplier' of rhythm and noise.**

Left: **An etching depicting a workshop for making instruments of times long past.**

Above: The shape of stringed instruments has changed over several centuries.

Right: Every violin-maker sticks his label in each instrument. This was how famous Italian masters signed themselves: Hieronymus Amati Cremonensis 1697, Antonius Stradivarius Cremonensis 1719, Guarneri 1697.

Above: Several generations of violin-makers lived in the Prague house 'Three Little Fiddlers', as its name implies.

Right: Let us compare the sizes of string instruments: violin 56–60 cm (22–23 ¹/₂ inches), viola 67–69 cm (26–27 inches) violoncello 124 cm (49 inches) and double bass 180–190 cm (71–75 inches).

Violin-makers also include those who build the cello and the double bass.

The manufacture of brass and percussion instruments about 1890.

sensitive hearing to discover the resonant qualities of the wood. When he has shaped the profile of both panels with fine tools, chisels and scrapers he will tap the pieces of wood and they will sound in intervals of fourths and fifths. Every time the violin-maker uses his scraper, his hand is guided by his idea of the future instrument; in his mind he can hear the high tone of the E-string and the low tone of the deeper G-string. It takes him several months to build a single instrument.

The very best resonant wood used to grow on the northern slopes of the Tyrolean Alps, at high altitudes in places with little sunshine. At that time—300 years ago—the air on our planet was pure and free of harmful pollution. Pine trees were felled in the winter, their trunks were left to rest for some time in the forest for the timber to dry out in a natural way. Then they were floated along mountain streams and from there along the River Po to the sea. The timber was then transported to the workshops of violin-makers in northern Italy, especially the towns of Brescia and Cremona.

The greatest of the master violin-makers of Cremona, **Antonio Stradivari** (1644–1737), is said to have built about 3,000 instruments. Some 600 of these have survived to this day. They cost vast sums of money and only the best-known violinists in the world are playing them. Stradivari even built an excellent violin when he was 93 years old; indeed, he stuck a label in it bearing his name and the comment '*anni* 93', his age at the time.

In terms of musical instruments, the towns of Brescia and Cremona have been bywords for excellence for a long time. For 150 years,

Niccolò Paganini, probably the greatest violinist of all times, a portrait painted by František Tichý.

The recorder

master instrument builders worked here and gave definite shape to violins, violas and violoncellos. To this day, their models are used as the pattern for constructing instruments, although their quality has never been equalled.

The first famous family of violin-makers in Cremona was the Amati family. After the founder of the dynasty, **Andrea Amati** (*c.* 1535–1611) came his famous grandson **Nicolo Amati** (1696–1684). All of the important violin-makers of Cremona, including Stradivari, trained or gained experience in his workshop. Another of Amati's pupils was **Andrea Guarneri** (*c.* 1626–98), the oldest of a noless famous family of violin-makers. His nephew, **Giuseppe Guarneri** (1687–1745), called 'del Gesù', whose violins can be compared with those of Stradivari, represented the summit of the classical era of Italian violin making. This period had been characterized by the original contributions made by the different families and the handing on of experience from generation to generation.

Other names and locations from the history of violin-making include the Tyrolean School, founded by **Jakob Stainer** (*c.* 1617–83), and the Prague School, from which came **Thomas Edlinger** (1622–1721). In 19th-century Paris, **Jean Baptiste Vaillaume** (1798–1875) gained fame from producing excellent copies of the old Italian master violin-makers.

Violins are complicated instruments with a carefully conceived construction to which no major changes have been made for 300 years. Many other instruments from the past have long since ceased to be played, but violins have survived the strain of the years and often constant use in concerts. That strain is no small matter: taut violin strings build up a pull of about 22 kilograms

Flute

Oboe

Bassoon

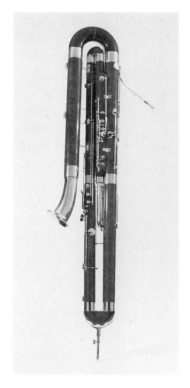

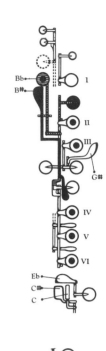

Double bassoon
       Clarinet
       Soprano saxophone

(48 pounds); the pressure of the bridge on the table of the violin is about 8 kilograms (18 pounds), and the table of the violin is only 2–5 millimetres ($^1/_{12}$ – $^1/_5$ inch) thick, even less in some places. All of this pressure is withstood by wood, the best-quality material supplied to us by nature.

Some national museums and private collections own rare instruments which are sometimes lent to outstanding artists. The most valuable of them have been valued at sums up to £1 million. There are strict rules for their use. They are transported in rigid containers and must not be placed in luggage compartments in planes or cars. (This is why a violoncello usually has its own plane ticket.) They require constant humidity and must not be exposed to extreme changes in temperature. This can create problems on concert tours abroad.

We tend to take it for granted that all stringed instruments are held in the left hand and the bow in the right. Nevertheless, this rule is not without exception. For example, the violinist **Rudolf Kolisch** (1896–1978), first violinist of the famous Austrian quartet bearing his name, lost one joint of his middle finger on the left hand in an accident in childhood. He learned to play the violin in an unusual way, holding it in his right hand and the bow in his left.

From Wood and Metal

It is freezing cold, outside a storm is raging and the wind is howling in the chimney. It is not a very pleasant sound and far from being harmonious, but even so there is something in its noise that is similar to music. The wind swirls the column of air inside the chimney; if it had blown quite regularly, at a steady speed, no doubt we should have heard a real musical tone.

Right: **A diagram of the mechanics of the flute and the clarinet.**

Alto saxophone

Above: **The saxophone provides the characteristic tone quality of a jazz band.**

Right: **The production of brass instruments in modern times.**

When you blow across the opening of a flute, the stream of expelled air strikes the edge of the opening and creates a regular vibration within. The longer the tube, the deeper the tone. When all the holes in the flute are covered, then its fundamental tone sounds. When the holes are gradually uncovered from the bottom upwards, the vibrating column of air is shortened and the flute produces a higher tone.

Our vocal chords are two tiny muscles that press together. Forcing air through them as you breathe out causes them to vibrate. The more firmly they press together, the higher the voice. An oboe or bassoon player presses a double reed, consisting of two small pieces of cane, between his lips and makes them vibrate with his breath. The vibration is transferred to the tube of the instrument and makes the air vibrate. The longer the instrument, the deeper the tone. The shortest double reed instrument is the oboe, with a high, soprano voice. The cor anglais or English horn is somewhat longer (in fact, it is the contralto oboe), the bassoon creates the tenor and baritone voices. The longest is the bass double bassoon. The tube of the double bassoon has to be coiled several times so that the player can manipulate the keys. If the double bassoon were to be straightened out, it would measure nearly 5 metres (17 feet). The clarinet functions in a similar manner. Its tone is produced by the vibration of a single reed set in the mouthpiece.

People have always used wood to build their homes and to make primitive weapons and household tools. It is also an excellent material for the making of wind instruments. Flutes are among the oldest, but the oboe and bassoon also have ancient predecessors. Their sounds were used by Bach and Handel and at the time of Mozart, the clarinet came into permanent use. In the 19th century, a whole family of woodwind instruments became an integral part of the Romantic orchestra.

To begin with, the woodwind instruments did not have valves; the

French horn

Bass trumpet

Trumpet

Trombone

Tuba

player simply covered the holes in the tube with his fingers. It was not until the beginning of the last century that a German instrument maker, **Theobald Boehm** (*c.* 1793–1881), perfected the fingering mechanism of these instruments with an ingenious system. His invention was used on the flute, the oboe and the clarinet.

The group of woodwind instruments was later joined by one other. It was constructed in 1840 in Paris by a Belgian instrument maker, **Adolphe Sax** (1814–94), and he christened it with his own name—the saxophone. Although the saxophone is made from metal in the same way as the flute, it is included with the woodwind. This may seem strange, but it is because the saxophone's construction and single reed is similar to that of the clarinet. There is a whole family of saxophones—

Right: **Two shapes for the mouthpiece: cup-shaped (for trumpet and trombone) and funnel-shaped (for French horn and tuba).**

sopranos, altos, tenors, baritones and bass. Even a sub-contrabass saxophone has been constructed, but this was rather a curiosity for an exhibition and copies can now only be found in museums. Saxophones belong to both classical and pop music. The saxophone was entirely at home in the jazz bands that sprang up in Europe in the 1920s in the American tradition; it even became a sort of symbol of this type of music.

Festive Brass

The blare of brass instruments gives a gloss to every festivity, both literally and figuratively: the sun is reflected off the polished metal and the stirring melodies are like an invitation, 'Come with us!' Their music will not make anyone sad.

There was a time when soldiers marching on the parade ground, or worse to war, were led by a brass band to help them keep in step on long, tiring marches and to make their burden of arms seem lighter. Sometimes they had a full band, at others a bugle and drums had to do. The sound of the bugle carried a long way—across the parade ground or the battlefield—and a repertoire of signals conveyed the orders of the commander.

Some musical instruments were also used during hunts. When the followers of the hunt were spread out in the depths of the forest, the huntsmen and the beaters communicated with each other by signals on horns. Once these were real animal horns, later they were replaced by metal tubes coiled into a circle and ending in a broad sounding bell.

Every large town had to have its trumpeters and the custom is pre-

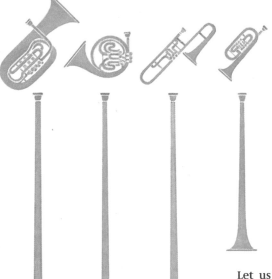

Let us compare the length of brass instruments. If the tubes of the instruments were unwound, they would measure: trumpet 132 cm (52 inches), trombone 271 cm (107 inches), French horn 372 cm (146 inches) and tuba 544 cm (214 inches).

The jazz trumpeter enjoys great popularity, almost as much as pop singers.

served to this day of trumpeters blowing a fanfare from tower galleries on solemn occasions.

In time, brass instruments found their way into orchestras, complementing the strings with their clarion call. For a long time, they were confined only to fanfares, sounding extended chords or rounding out the overall sound of the orchestra. This is because, in its original form—fitted with a reed by which the lips of the player set the air inside the instrument in regular vibration—the metal instrument could only play a limited number of natural tones. It was not until the instrument was fitted first with keys and later with valves that it could equal other instruments and was able to play a true melody.

Every symphony orchestra now has brass instruments, of which there are four basic ones: the bugle, the French horn, the trombone and the tuba.

A group of French horns is capable of conjuring up the romantic mood of a sombre forest, such as in the overture to Weber's *Der Freischütz.* Sometimes the bugle stirs the memory of its original function, when it was used to convey military signals. Thus in Beethoven's *Leonora* overture Number 3, there is a typical example and in the opening movement of Janáček's *Sinfonietta*, a group of bugles blares out in full splendour.

The Baroque era was already acquainted with the skilful art of trumpeters, although they played on a different instrument called the clarinet, a long, simple tube on which it was possible to play even exacting parts at high pitch. For example, Bach's second *Brandenburg Concerto* is not an easy piece, even for the modern soloist.

Tabulature—record of music from the 16th century. Compositions for the lute are not written in notes but in finger touches and rhythm.

The harpsichord. A historic instrument among the memorabilia of Mozart (Bertramka Villa, Prague).

Joseph Haydn dedicated his well-known Concerto in E flat major to the inventor of the valve trumpet. For the first time, Haydn was able to write not only brisk fanfare melodies, but also melodic chromatic movements for the trumpet. The modern trumpet has achieved unusual popularity in jazz and dance music, a place it still holds. The uncrowned king of this instrument was undoubtedly **Louis Armstrong** (1900—71).

The Harp and the Harpsichord

A hundred and fifty years ago, it seemed that the harpsichord had reached the end of its days, with instruments lying unplayed in museums. It was only at the beginning of this century that musicians found new interest in this keyboard instrument. Why not play Baroque and Classical musical on the instruments for which they had been written. So once again, the soft tones of the harpsichord were heard in solo, chamber and concert pieces of Bach, Handel, Domenico Scarlatti (1685–1757), Jean-Philippe Rameau (1683–1764), and François Couperin (1668–1733). Today, the harpsichord is once again a fully-fledged member of the instrumental family and new ones are being constructed based on those that have been preserved. Modern composers are even writing for the harpsichord.

The harp and harpsichord are distant relatives. The strings of a harp are sounded by being plucked (the harpist uses only four fingers of each hand, the little finger is not used). The strings of the harpsichord are also plucked, although not directly by the fingers. Originally a raven's quill and now a special plectrum is linked to the keyboard by an upright piece of wood. Large instruments have two keyboards, manuals, and so also two systems of strings. The two-manual makes it possible to play clearly differentiated polyphonic sounds and to alternate tone colour and loudness and softness. Unlike the piano, the harpsichord cannot achieve continuous amplifying or decreasing of sound; its dynamism is terrace-like, as in the Baroque organ. Another difference from the modern piano is that the top keyboard of the harpsichord is white and the bottom is black.

The harp is one of the oldest instruments. David is mentioned as playing the harp in the Bible. It was known to the Egyptians, and

The harp, as we know it today, and its Egyptian predecessor.

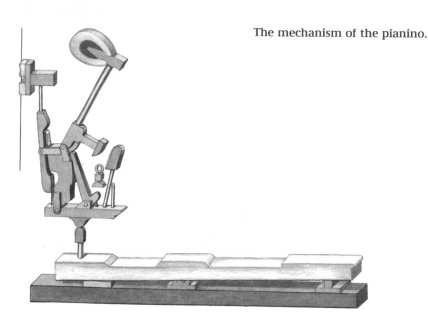

The mechanism of the pianino.

a tangent, strikes the st- ⌐g, shortening it to the required ⌐ngth and making it vibrate. This instrument has a very delicate tone and compositions were written for it by Bach and his contemporaries. It was later overtaken by the harpsichord and more especially by the pianoforte.

The Pianoforte or Fortepiano

The dulcimer is generally assumed to be a folk instrument from somewhere in the east which came to Europe in the Middle Ages. It is often thought of as being at home somewhere on the periphery of

Frédéric Chopin and Franz Liszt, two of the greatest pianists of the 19th century.

A view of a workshop in which pianos are manufactured.

was very popular in the Middle Ages. Wandering musicians took their harps from town to town, playing in taverns and later in better-class households. It was the romantic 19th century that brought the harp to the concert stage, where it became the instrument of virtuosi as well as the adornment of the symphony orchestra. It was

provided with a complex mechanism allowing it to be played in all tones.

Another early instrument, related to the harpsichord, that is coming back into use after more than 200 years, is the clavichord. The clavichord's strings run at right angles to the keys. When a key is depressed, a metal tongue, called

Right: A modern grand piano — widely used and never out of date.

Right: A modern grand piano — widely used and never out of date.

the music world, probably in an ale house near the Balaton Lake in Hungary, where it is known as the cimbalom. In fact, it is a sort of great-grandfather of the modern piano, a universal instrument of many possibilities.

The harpsichord is incapable of loud or soft shading of tone. Whether we strike the key of a harpsichord strongly of gently, it has no effect on the strength of the tone. Instrument-makers looked for ways of getting around this problem and the first to succeed was an Italian, Bartolomeo Cristofori, at the beginning of the 18th century. He did this by replacing the plucking mechanism of the harpsichord with hammers connected to a keyboard. His invention was then perfected by a German, Gottfried Silbermann (1683–1753).

As the new instrument was capable of playing both softly and loudly, it was called in Italian *stromento col piano e forte.* The name stuck and was shortened and turned round to become pianoforte, fortepiano, or just the abbreviated piano.

Its rivalry with the harpsichord lasted for 100 years. In the end, the hammer piano was the absolute victor. Mozart and Beethoven composed for it, but it was Liszt, Chopin, Clara Schumann (1819–1896) and their contemporaries who raised the piano to its full glory. This was at the time when the performance of music was shifting from the salons of the aristocracy to bigger and bigger concert halls and when the virtuoso was becoming the centre of inter-

Rudolf Firkušný, one of the gallery of famous pianists of modern times.

The upright piano, the forerunner of the pianino, dating from the beginning of the 19th century.

Above: **Sheng**—a Chinese wind instrument, a sort of rudimentary organ.

Right: **A religious concert with the organ at the time of Bach.**

est in society, the admired and pampered darling who could be envied even by today's pop stars. Crowds of cheering admirers awaited the artist in his dressing-room and students would unharness the horses and pull the maestro's carriage through the applauding crowds lining the streets.

Large halls called for new and more powerful instruments whose tones would carry and whose mechanism would resist pressure unknown until then in the world of music. It is a fact that a piano collapsed under the hands of Liszt and the soft iron strings snapped.

So piano manufacturers built better and better instruments until they arrived at the models that are being produced today in an almost unchanged form. Among these were the Viennese company

Bösendorfer, the Parisian firm of Sebastian Erard, Blüthner from Leipzig, Bechstein from Berlin and Petrof and Förster from Bohemia. The best pianos were made by the Steinway company in New York and its name became world famous. New trade names are still appearing, among them the Japanese Yamaha is well to the fore.

The piano is not intended only for the concert stage. It is widespread, necessary everywhere: in schools, dance bands, theatres (as an essential aid to the conductor and the singing coach) and as an instrument for music-making in the home. Many small homes have a small upright piano or pianino. The forerunner of this appeared in various types of upright pianos, for instance the 'giraffe' piano, or the 'pyramid' piano be-

fore it finally crystallized into the universal shape known today.

A Royal Instrument

When Johann Sebastian Bach tried out a new organ, he always began by pulling out all the stops and playing the instrument at full strength. He would say that he had to find out first of all what sort of lungs the organ had. Only then, would he play over the individual registers and their combinations, listen to the contrasts of tone and dynamism between the different manuals and the pedal. He learned how the mechanism reacted to the movement of hand or foot and how the link between the keys and the pipes worked. Bach was unequalled as an organist and had no rival in his mastery of the art. People came to Leipzig from afar to hear him play in St Thomas's church.

The organ is a complicated music machine. It comprises three main parts: the bellows, or the lungs of the organ, usually concealed from sight, the pipes and the manual. The pipes, metal or wooden, are placed in rows, or flue stops, each supplying a particular tone quality and strength. Using different stops and playing on two or more manuals and pedals alternates tone qualities and loud and soft shades. Above all, it is possible to achieve distinct polyphony. In small organs, the console, the brain of the whole instru-

Let us take a look at the complicated mechanism of a Baroque organ.

(1) Front positive (the rank of pipes in the front part of the gallery)
(2) Rank of metal pipes
(3) Wooden pipes
(4) Pipe column
(5) Console
(6) First manual (1st keyboard)
(7) Second manual (2nd keyboard)
(8) Pedal (pedal keyboard)
(9) Mechanical traction of pedal
(10) Stop button
(11) Bellows
(12) Air duct to the front positive

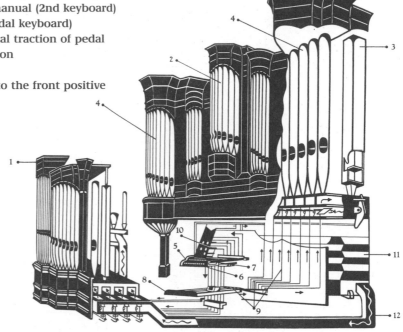

The organ of a Baroque church. The picture conjures up the noble sound that echoes through the large space.

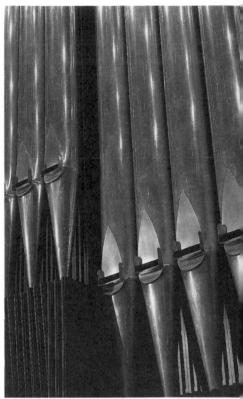

Detail of organ pipes.

Over the centuries, the organ has changed its external appearance, too, adjusting to modern architecture. It has always been placed in the main part of the church as a counterbalance to the altar. The music pours down from the gallery as if from heavenly heights, the organ being hidden from the sight of the congregation. In modern concert halls, on the other hand, the organ dominates the stage. The audience not only hears its sound but sees the shape of the instrument and can observe the player.

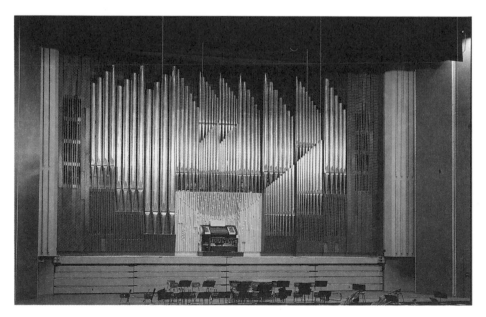

ment, has only one manual but two or three are more usual and a large organ has five. The largest organ in the world was built in Atlantic City in the United States. It has seven manuals, 938 stops and 33,114 pipes.

The interaction between the console and the pipes is achieved by a system of levers and rods (trackers and stickers)—the traction. In the 19th century, the original mechanism of the traction was replaced by new systems, for instance, pneumatic levers to transmit the impulses from the consoles to the pipe valves.

Later, electricity intervened in the development of organ building and an electric motor has eliminated the effort of working the bellows by foot pressure. The main thing, however, was that electricity connected the entire control system. The console can now be placed at some distance from the instrument itself. In recent decades, advanced electronics have been used to make it possible to programme a number of sound combinations from the manuals which can then be incorporated by the simple pressing of a button. At the moment, organ builders are returning to the mechanical system, perfected, however, by modern technology. The priority is to achieve direct contact between the player and the instrument.

Organs have also developed in their sound image. In the 19th century, in harmony with the romantic mood, new stop voices were introduced. The organ was supposed to replace all instruments; it was to become a sort of symphonic orchestra for a single player. This was undoubtedly a failure because the original classical character of the organ was lost. Now, the Baroque ideal of sound is once more being sought. Modern instruments are being built with a selection of voices, or dispositions, which will make it possible to reproduce the music of all periods and styles in their appropriate sounds.

Building an organ starts on the table of the designer, with calculations of acoustics, establishment of the number and selection of tones and suggestions for external shape. The organ builders work in close co-operation with musicians. There are no two instruments in the world that are exactly the same. Each space requires a different selection of stops, a different size of instrument and different design.

In the past, master organ-builders travelled from town to town with their workmen and all their equipment. Organs are now built in workshops. After being tested, they are taken apart and then re-assembled on site. Even now, designers of modern organs are inspired by the sound and technical solutions given to the instruments by their ancestors, in particular the masters of the Baroque era. The engineer Gottfried Silbermann was mentioned in connection with the invention of the piano. He must be mentioned again as one of the most important organ-builders whose instruments we admire to this day.

From Organ to Synthesizer

The music of the 20th century has been marked by the invention of the microphone, the amplifier and the loudspeaker. The feeble sound of the harpsichord, which was intended to be played in the salons of country houses or in the town houses of burghers, can today be amplified with simple equipment so that it will fill a concert hall. Most pop singers could hardly appear on stage without the microphone; with it, their sometimes extremely weak voices can now fill the largest concert hall or stadium.

Classic guitar

The electric guitar does not need a sound box like the acoustic guitar. This is replaced by the amplifier.

Synthesizers have brought a remarkable enrichment of sound to musical instruments, but have not entirely replaced classical instruments.

Electricity has also made it possible to invent entirely new instruments or to develop others from traditional instruments. This takes place by transforming acoustic sound waves into the analogous flow of an electric current, which, after being boosted, is changed into audible sound in the loudspeakers. The volume and depth of the tone can be adjusted at will and its timbre can be changed by the addition of filters.

There are now three main groups of such instruments. Chief among them are the electro-acoustic instruments, in which an existing instrument is connected to an electro-acoustic transformer, such as a microphone, and the original weak signal is then further processed. In the 1930s, this process was already used in the invention of the Neo-Bechstein electrical piano, in which the soundboard, or resonator, was replaced by an electromagnetic pick-up. In the 1960s, the electro-acoustical guitar spread dramatically. It was with this that The Beatles first won fame. An insignificant instrument with no resonating body can give out a stronger sound than an entire symphonic orchestra.

The second group is electrophonic instruments. In these, electrical vibrations are activated by turning cog wheels, the generators. The electric current is then transformed into acoustic values. This principle was used to construct electrophonic organs, manufactured by the American firm Hammond. To some degree they were able to replace the sound of the classical organ and the arrangement of their consoles was also derived from the organ. They were used mostly in pop music.

Developments over the past few decades have been towards electronic instruments, of which the most versatile are synthesizers. Their tone is produced by purely electronic means and they can produce innumerable tone combinations beyond the scope of any other existing instruments. Synthesizers can be easily mastered; even unskilful musicians can quickly learn to use them. This is why they are widely used in pop music and in rock bands. Composers of serious music, however, are also taking advantage of the synthesizer's versatility.

Canned Music

Unfulfilled Dreams

We now take it for granted that we can preserve any sound at all and bring it to life again whenever we like. In our absence, the telephone will record messages and we can record our favourite pieces from the radio. Like the food we placed in the freezer several months ago from which we shall make a meal today, we simply close up the sounds in 'cans' to preserve them.

Attempts to preserve sound for a long time or to carry it from one place to another are as old as humanity itself. It is not surprising that people have long been trying to do this, both in their imagination and in actual experiments. For example, François Rabelais's novel *Gargantua and Pantagruel* describes balls of ice in which human voices were said to be frozen; unfortunately no one understood them because they spoke a barbaric language. One of the most fantastic stories was an adventure that the famous Baron Münchhausen was said to have experienced on one of his journeys. During a severe frost, the sound of a coachman's horn froze; only when he hung the horn near the fire in a tavern did the sound ring out!

Written Sound

Thousands of years had to pass before people discovered a way to record sound and reproduce it again. On the other hand, they fairly quickly found a way first to preserve words, and then music and song in writing, so we can, at least, in part discover how the music of our ancestors sounded.

Literature is the main written relic that survives from antiquity. Although we know the Greek tragedies and can see them on the modern stage after more than 2,000 years, we can only guess how the choir that sang in the Greek theatre sounded. One of the few musical relics from antiquity is a funeral song inscribed on the tombstone of a man called Seikilos. It was found not far from Smyrna in Asia Minor. Signs above the Greek letters indicate the height of the tones.

The Middle Ages provided us with a richer source of information, although the notation of the liturgical songs and chorales is not very intelligible at first sight. Special signs—neums—indicated the approximate direction of the melody and acted as a support of the singer's memory. Church hymns were mainly preserved as oral tradition.

As time went on, written notes developed into an increasingly clear form until they not only

We don't know whether the dog really recognized his master's voice on the record. Whatever the case, he became the symbol for a gramophone record company.

recorded the height of the tone but also its rhythmic course. The line system was gradually introduced and this set the height of the tone precisely. At first there were four lines, later five. Two used to be coloured and determined the tones F and C. At the beginning of the staff a letter was written, which in time developed into the clef (F is used for the bass, C for the alto or the tenor). The present-day, complicated score for an orchestral composition is thus the result of the development of notation over a very long time.

Printed Music

Printed sheet music also passed through a long period of development. At first only the lines were printed in hymn books and the notes had to be written in by hand. Then an entire page was engraved on a wooden panel from which prints were made on a printer's press. Later, the notes were written on a copper plate with an engraving tool and a printing matrix was made from this. Some composers, such as

Above: **The text and melody of a funeral hymn are inscribed on Seikilos's tombstone.**

Right: **The clefs originated from their initial labelling with letters (G clef—violin, C clef—alto and tenor, F clef—bass).**

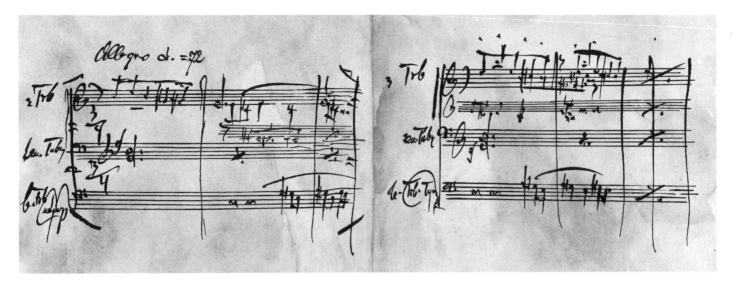

Copyists had a difficult time with the hand written scores of Leoš Janáček. The picture shows an excerpt from the first movement of his *Sinfonietta*.

Bach, transcribed their own works in this way. As in book printing, great progress came with the typesetting of notes. Gottlob Immanuel Breitkopf, a printer from Leipzig (1719–94), founder of the well-known publishing house Breitkopf and Härtel, played an important part in the development of this technique.

The 19th century brought the invention of lithography, which then predominated in music printing as well. However, without doubt, by far the most perfect, although the most laborious method was engraving notes. An entire sheet of music is engraved and die-stamped on to a zinc panel. The engraver uses about 60 dies for the different kinds of notes and signs, rests and clefs, to indicate loudness and softness and so on. It takes a skilled engraver from eight to ten hours to complete a sheet

Left: **The first page of the score for Benjamin Britten's** *Young Person's Guide to the Orchestra* **(variation and fugue on a theme of Henry Purcell). Each instrument has its line and the voices of the instruments are written in order: woodwind, brass, percussion, harp, strings.**

of music, longer if the score is complex. Although new methods of printing music have been discovered that are cheaper and less laborious, engraving is still used because of its graphic perfection. The onerous work of a note engraver can only be replaced by the modern computer, which is able to read the author's manuscript and transcribe it into clear, well-arranged print.

The composer must still write his notes by hand, using a pen and paper marked with the five-lined staff. Although a typewriter for musical notation has been invented, it is not widely used.

Toys for Enjoyment

The old-fashioned alarm clock that works on a spring mechanism is, in fact, a simple computer. If we put the time it should wake us up into its memory, it rings reliably. Regularly, every day, it repeats the sound that we want, although sometimes reluctantly, to hear. The Persian King Xerxes had a special slave who mechanically repeated every morning the single sentence, 'My lord, do not forget Athens!'

To repeat a sound, to have a sound signal to hand, was a need that people felt long, long ago. For example, they attempted to reproduce human speech or the

The note printer. Note by note, sign by sign, the engraver cuts or hammers them into a zinc plate, in negative, from right to left. It takes him between eight and ten hours to complete one page of a score.

sounds of animals artificially. In the 19th century, craftsmen produced many ingenious toys making sounds that brought great advances in the field of mechanics. Some of them, such as talking dolls, calling geese and barking dogs, have survived. Attempts were also made to make a real, mechanical copy of human speech. Complicated apparatus was constructed and the inventors presented a great variety of speaking and singing figures at fairs and at solemn assemblies. The beautiful Olympia, a puppet who was indistinguishable from a living person, even appeared on stage in one of the *Tales of Hoffmann* by Offenbach.

Who does not enjoy having a little music at home? At the time when the radio and stereo were still in the distant future and not many could afford to maintain their own orchestras, mechanical music boxes, music machines and musical clocks were produced for home use. At the press of a button or the pulling of a string, an operatic aria, a patriotic air, a street song, a famous waltz or military march would fill the room. Well-known tunes were al-

Below: In 1825 Louis Braille composed a system of raised dots for writing for the blind. A combination of six raised dots can be used to write all letters, numbers and notes or supporting musical symbols. This is how clefs may be written.

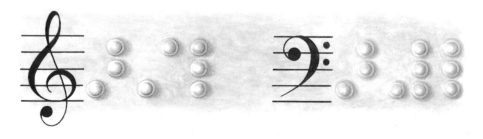

so heard in the streets from barrel organs. In restaurants, orchestrions were played and, later, pianos driven by electricity. Anybody could 'play' these instruments without being able to read music. New compositions were even written for these music machines, Beethoven himself composed a piece in 1813 for the music machine of the mechanic J. N. Mälzel, the inventor of the metronome; called 'Wellington's Victory', or 'The Battle at Vittorie', it was not his best composition.

More Serious Experiments

Inventors never tired in their efforts to capture and reproduce real music. Several methods were devised for recording piano music, for example. The firm Welte in Germany got furthest and it is thanks to them that we now have access to unique recordings of famous pianists from the beginning of the 20th century. A complicated mechanism was built into a Steinway piano. A moving paper strip registered the composition being played, with all its shades of dynamics and tempo. So, today, we can listen to Debussy, Grieg, Saint-Saëns, Strauss, Ravel, Busoni and a number of other maestros. These documentary recordings have been reconstructed and reissued on LP records and CDs.

A Prophesy

When I opened the casket containing the talking book, I found there something metal that looked like the works of our clock. It was full of I don't know what sort of little springs and incomprehensible cogwheels. It is a real book and you don't need eyes but ears to get acquainted with its contents. When anyone wants to read he must taut-

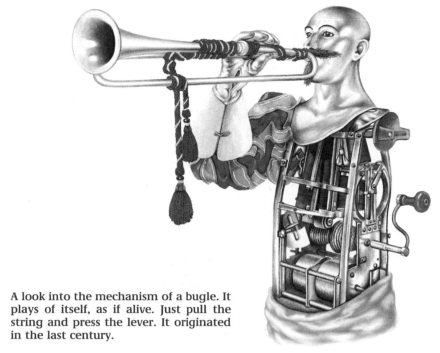

A look into the mechanism of a bugle. It plays of itself, as if alive. Just pull the string and press the lever. It originated in the last century.

The orchestrion, a mechanical instrument with organ pipes and brass instruments.

From the early history of sound recording: the vibration of the sound element is inscribed as a graph on a revolving cylinder. These experiments led to the phonograph and the gramophone.

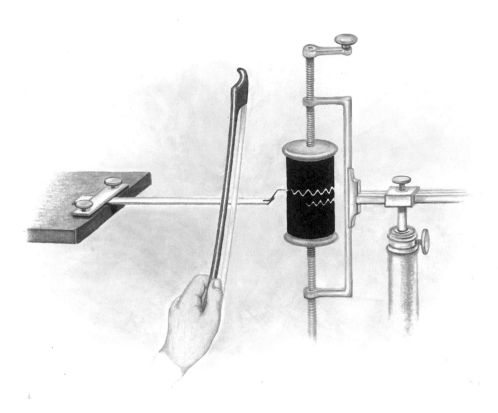

en a large number of the most varied thin fibres and then turn an arrow towards the chapter he wants to listen to. At once, clear sounds emerge as from a human mouth or a musical instrument which have the function of speech. When I pondered over this strange invention, I was no longer surprised that the young men of this country have greater knowledge at the age of 16 or 18 than our grey-haired old men. For they are never without their lessons, either at home or out walking, whether in the town or on their travels. They can carry as many as thirty such books in their pockets.

Does this remind you of the personal stereo that you carry in your pocket, bag or brief case? Perhaps you use it to listen to a language course or the latest pop songs. Only the style is a little strange — and some of the details seem rather suspicious. This forecast of

Thomas Alva Edison (1847–1931), the ingenious inventor of the phonograph.

Thanks to new inventions, even children's toys started to speak. What is the doll saying? What interests the monkey on the phonograph? And what could be in the box containing the phonograph cylinder?

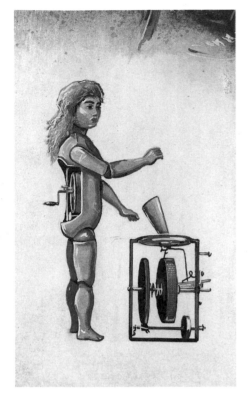

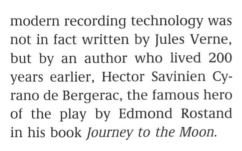

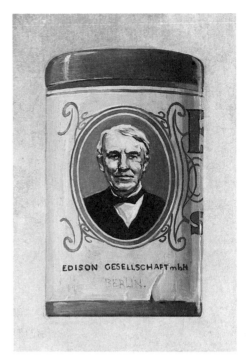

modern recording technology was not in fact written by Jules Verne, but by an author who lived 200 years earlier, Hector Savinien Cyrano de Bergerac, the famous hero of the play by Edmond Rostand in his book *Journey to the Moon.*

The Phonograph and the Gramophone

Realizing the dream of recording sound required an investigation into the physical properties of sound. In 1877, the American inventor Thomas Alva Edison, while reciting the simple nursery rhyme, 'Mary Had a Little Lamb', in his laboratory in Menlo Park, was able to hear his voice reproduced on the grooves on a rotating cylinder covered with aluminium foil. He had made the first great breakthrough. Before this, however, it

was necessary to discover that sound spreading through the air makes a membrane vibrate and that, with the help of a spring, the vibration can be transferred to a writing nib, making a graph on a blackened surface that is an 'image' of the sound wave.

These experiments were made in the first half of the 19th century. It was Edison who succeeded—by chance—in recording the sound with a needle in soft material and then reviving it again. He called his apparatus a phonograph and unwittingly opened up a new epoch in the advance of musical culture. Edison's phonograph became the sensation of the day. At first, it was meant to be used as a dictaphone. The recording was imperfect and could be replayed only a few times, sometimes even only once.

It was not until aluminium foil was replaced by a firmer material and the cylinders were produced industrially that the phonograph could record music. At the turn of the century, the phonograph was used to record the voices of famous singers. The recordings were faulty but they have immense historical value. The phonograph helped to preserve the disappearing art of folk singers in the villages as well and have also been used to study social history.

The heirs to Edison were the Frenchman Charles Cros and the German Emil Berliner, who in 1887 replaced the cylinder with a flat disc; basically the same as used on modern record players. Instead of recording sound waves in depth, Berliner used a 'sideways' recording in which the needle described a graph formed into a spiral running from the edge to the centre of the disc. In contrast to the cylinder, the disc could be easily duplicated by pressing an almost unlimited number.

Above: **A phonograph with a large fly-wheel which maintained the regular revolutions of the cylinder.**

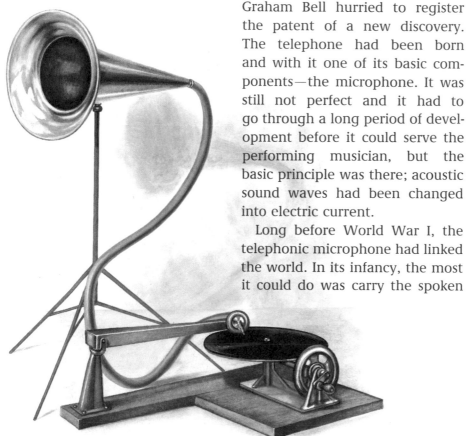

Berliner's gramophone.

The Electric Ear

'Mr Watson! Come here! I want you!' Mr Bell calls into a peculiar machine to summon the help of his assistant because he has just spilled sulphuric acid on himself.

This was the first sentence ever carried on the path of electricity. The year was 1876. Alexander Graham Bell hurried to register the patent of a new discovery. The telephone had been born and with it one of its basic components—the microphone. It was still not perfect and it had to go through a long period of development before it could serve the performing musician, but the basic principle was there; acoustic sound waves had been changed into electric current.

Long before World War I, the telephonic microphone had linked the world. In its infancy, the most it could do was carry the spoken voice; its frequency range did not come close to that required for the relay of the sound of musical instruments or the singing voice. For a long time, people spoke and sang into the funnel of the phonograph or the gramophone, the needle mechanically linked to the membrane, cutting a groove in the rotating cylinder or disc. Voices were distorted, musical instruments were unrecognizable. Although the sound could be reproduced mechanically, it could only be magnified by large baffles connected to amplifiers.

The basic principle of the microphone had yet to be worked out and the invention of an electronic amplifier capable of transferring electrical impulses into recording equipment was still to come. This happened in the mid-1920s. Electrical recording produced a gramophone disc that had a fairly true reproduction capability on which it was possible to capture, with the help of one or more microphones, not only the performance of a singer or a solo instrument with accompaniment, but also a full ensemble of instruments, a dance band or a symphonic orchestra. The recording was made electrically. The sound was played back making mechanical bleating sounds on a gramophone driven by a spring. It was only later that electrical play-backs came into use.

The modern recording industry expanded dramatically. Large-scale symphonic works and entire operas were recorded. There was still, however, one major obstacle; one side of a large disc, 30 centimetres (12 inches) in diameter, with a standard 78 rotations a minute, could take five minutes of recording at the most. Longer pieces had to be cut into small sections and the listener had to turn over or change the disc (and also the needle) every five minutes. For instance, the recording of a two-hour opera, such as Verdi's *Rigoletto*, was issued by Columbia on 15 discs divided into 30 sections. Smaller discs, 25 centimetres (10 inches) in diameter, could take only three minutes, something that had a significant influence on the production of pop music. Songs and dance music were composed according to these technical dimensions. Johann Strauss did not have such limitations in the previous century; he could write his waltzes without any restrictions on their length.

Thanks to gramophone records, good-quality operatic, chamber and symphonic music was soon available to the general public. The pop industry enjoyed unusual expansion. Records introduced Europe to American jazz and spread this new musical style.

The Tape Recorder

The principle of recording sound on tape dates back some time. Its creator was Valdemar Poulsen, a Danish engineer who presented his invention at the World Exhibition in Paris in 1900. However, it was not until the mid-1930s that the tape recorder gradually came into use in radio, where it was capable of recording and reproducing not only important spoken but also musical programmes. After World War II the tape recorder was also used in record production and had a marked influence on this field.

The tape recorder arrived at the same time as the introduction of the long-playing disc, or LP, which was first put on the market in 1948 by Columbia. Unlike older records that were made of brittle material, the new discs were more durable, less prone to damage and ran at a speed of 33⅓ rotations per minute. They had finer, more densely packed grooves, so one side could incorporate a programme of up to 25 minutes.

The introduction of the tape recorder into radio and the record industry was of far-reaching importance in terms of improving the quality of artistic interpretation. The musician in the studio was no longer restricted to recording a single and, he hoped, flawless performance. He could repeat the composition several times and faulty passages could be replaced by better ones. The tapes could be cut and the recording could be improved technically. This did not mean the work of the artist was any easier. On the contrary, the high quality of recording expected by the public today means that much greater demands are imposed on the artist, both in the recording studio and at concerts.

The tape recorder made possible what is now commonplace: stereophonic recording and reproduction. From initial experiments in which the listener heard sound

A phonograph for both ears—or for two listeners.

Right: Producers competed in the improvement of the mechanics of amplifiers and gramophone cabinets with large amplifiers. But what did it signify? Before World War I there was still a long way to go to hifi sound.

143

effects coming from the right or the left—like watching the bouncing ball in table tennis—we arrived at a modern concept in which the main concern is to reproduce faithfully the scope of the sound. Even in a small room, we can now achieve the illusion of listening to music in a large concert hall.

In the sphere of pop music, the arrival of the tape recorder offered new and exciting opportunities. Today, songs are recorded in succession on many-channelled tape recorders, with 16 or more sound tracks separately recording the rhythm instruments and the melody sections. Only when this background has been prepared does the singer come on to the scene to record his part, and he can do this by singing in three different voices, one after the other. The sound director then mixes all the separate parts of the recording on the mixing panel to produce the final sound.

While with classical music the aim is to record as faithfully as possible what the listeners hear in the concert hall without electrical amplification, in pop music the composer or arranger knows in advance that the final version of the composition will be achieved in the studio, and that he will have to adjust the timbre of the instruments in relation to their loudness or softness. This could not possibly be done without electro-acoustic adjustment.

Tape recording has also influenced 'live' performances of pop music. Many players and singers on stage 'fake' their exhausting performance. The audience is, in fact, listening to a recording that was prepared long before in the recording studio, played through loud-speakers.

One remarkable form of recording and reproduction is quadrophonics. Here, the microphone records sound from four different points and four loud-speakers, carefully placed in the room where the recording is heard, create the perfect illusion of a concert hall. Without realizing it, we are hearing, in addition to the direct sound, the reflection of sound waves from the side walls of the room and from the wall behind the listeners.

Music for Tape

Over the past few decades, the tape recorder and the development of electronics have made it possible not only to improve sound recording and the faithful reproduction of a musical work, but they have also opened up an entirely new branch of musical composition.

Music that is shaped in the electro-acoustic studio without using classical instruments does not result in a musical score that has to be brought to life by musicians; it produces a tape. This type of sound production—which is entirely different from what for centuries we have called music—is used as scenic music in the theatre, in TV, films and as a creation in itself, intended to be heard at public performances or at home. One of the founders of this new branch of music is the French composer and theoretician **Pierre Schaeffer** (b. 1910).

There are two basic trends in this field of sound art. Specific music is produced by the refashioning of real sound, whether musical or non-musical, which is 'caught' by a microphone on to a tape and then rearranged electronically in various ways. As an example, let us take the simplest way. We can play the tape recording backwards, change the speed of the tape, cut out various sounds and passages and arrange them to make an interesting sound formation. The other trend is electronic music, in which all the sounds are created completely artificially and arranged on electro-acoustic equipment. The material of electro-acoustic music is no longer our customary tone system, because

The tape recorder made the play-back possible. The singer, wearing earphones, listens to the earlier recording on tape of the instrumental accompaniment. The final recording results from linking the singing voice to the accompaniment.

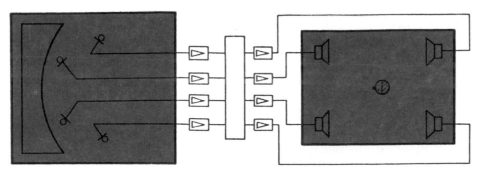

The principle of quadrophonic transmission: four microphones are placed in the recording studio (on the left), two in the front, directed towards the musicians and two at the back, taking the sound from space as it is reflected from the walls; four independent routes of transmission lead to four reproductors in the auditorium (on the right).

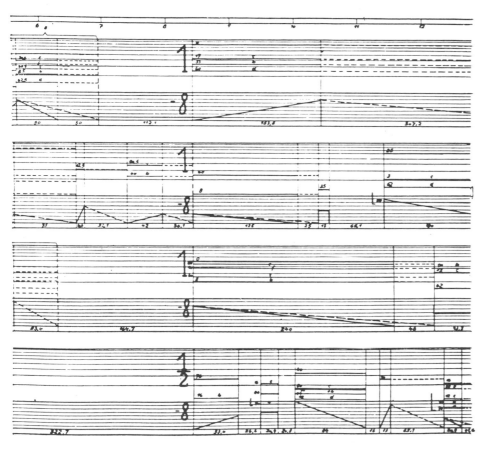

The score of an electro-acoustic composition.

highest audible frequency, a tension sample is scanned that is coded into the binary system as 0 or 1, and recorded on to the tape. From here, through a complicated production process, it is transferred to the compact disc. These 0s and 1s are recorded as microscopic pits on the disc in spirals running from the centre to the edge. They are scanned by a laser beam, and other equipment once again transposes them into audible sound. The size of the pits is expressed in thousandths of a millimetre. A total of 250,000 pits can be accommodated on 1 square millimetre. The disc revolves at a speed of 500 to 250 revolutions per minute, its speed reducing from the centre to the edge of the disc, thus the same speed at the outer edge as at the centre is maintained.

So much for the basic theory.

Below: The latest stage in the technology of sound recording—the compact disc.

by using electricity, tones of different frequencies and absolutely new sound timbre can be created that can never be achieved on classical instruments. The composer creates such music in close co-operation with a technical specialist.

DIGI and CD

The impact of digital recording, or DIGI, and the compact disc, or CD, is colossal—their importance is so revolutionary that this leap in technology can perhaps be compared only with Gutenberg's invention of book printing.

Computers have broken into music. The course of sound waves, and so electrical tension, can be converted into a numerical code. At a minimum of 40,000 times a second, which is double the

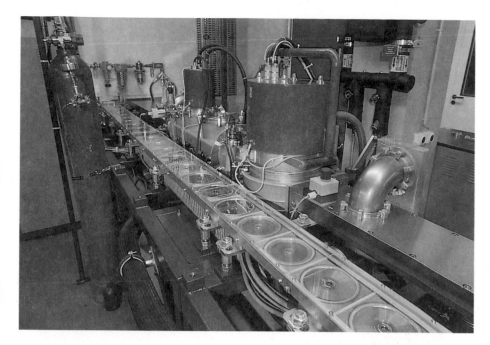

The CD is produced in an environment that is meticulously protected from dust.

What about the results? The CD can hold almost 80 minutes of music (remember those 15 records that were needed to accommodate a two-hour opera), it eliminates all kinds of disturbing murmur and it captures a dynamic range that previous records and tapes were incapable of doing. There is nothing more to desire.

A compact disc can hold a gigantic amount of information—not just music. One side can hold 200,000 pages of typewritten text; 24 volumes of the *Encyclopaedia Britannica* can be recorded on a single disc; and one side can hold up to 12 hours of speech. Cyrano de Bergerac would be very surprised to learn how far our modern technology has outstripped his fantastic prophesy.

Through the World of Music

In the pages of this book, we have tried to take part in a speeded-up journey around the world. Sometimes we have paused a while and looked around us, at others, we were only to fly over a country and observe it from a distance. We discovered how the world of music is dependent on our world, is a mirror for it and how music conveys our feelings and thoughts. We have seen how music depicts human happenings—some of them real, some imaginary—and how, through its own special means, it creates its own life developing in parallel with the life of human society.

On our map of the world of music there are still two places that we should not pass over without a glance.

People and Machinery

It was a fortunate decade that followed World War I, when technical progress was running at full speed and when human ingenuity, skill and endurance exceeded the previously unsurpassed limits of human capability. Let us recall a few facts: advances in aviation; the automobile industry; radio-technology; cinema; new sporting records; architecture relieved of

A still life by Georges Braque, one of the artists who determined the course of modern art in the 20th century.

senseless ornamentation; new construction techniques with simple lines and well-designed interiors for the urban environment.

1922 Johnny Weissmüller was the first person to swim 100 metres (330 feet) free-style in under one minute.

The BBC was the first station in the world to inaugurate regular radio broadcasting.

1924 An Alfa Romeo racing car in the Italian Grande Prix at Mons travelled at an average speed of 168 kilometres (105 miles) per hour.

1927 Charles Lindberg was the first to fly from New York to Paris non-stop in 33 hours.

1928 General Nobile flew over the North Pole in the 'Italia'. On the way back his expedition crashed.

The steam locomotives achieved a speed of 120 kilometres (75 miles) per hour.

The city spread out beneath the Eiffel Tower was always fertile soil for the encouragement of new trends in the arts.

Pacific 231, **the first page of a score by Arthur Honegger.**

Above: **The Paris Six, a famous group of artists with modern orientation. They were the composers Darius Milhaud, Arthur Honegger, Francis Poulenc, Georges Auric, Germaine Tailleferre, Louis Edmond Durey and the poet Jean Cocteau.**

Martinů Half-time · La Bagarre · Intermezzo
Thunderbolt P-47 · The Rock
Brno State Philharmonic Orchestra · Petr Vronský

The painting by Kamil Lhoták (1912–90) on the sleeve of a record of Bohuslav Martinů's compositions reflects and expresses the composer's enchantment with the world of technology.

The architecture of the 1920s was seeking new directions, along with other branches of the arts. This can be seen from the use of new technical possibilities in the construction of buildings, a more effective arrangement of interior space and the simplified shapes of buildings. The picture shows the coffee house and terraces at Barrandov, Prague, by the architect Max Urban.

Professor Piccard prepared to rise in a balloon into the stratosphere; the world was able to enjoy the great talent of Charlie Chaplin on the film screen. Radio stations linked up the world with speedy information and carried both classical and light music into people's homes, with the turn of a knob. A new kind of music, namely jazz, took Europe by storm. Sports stadia were filled with thousands of spectators.

Musical composition reacted to the new atmosphere. A group of composers, 'Les Six', were operating in Paris. Their music reflected the times and an admiration of technology. They experienced the excitement of sport and they accepted jazz inspiration for their music. One member of the group, Arthur Honegger, wrote a symphonic movement, *Pacific 231* (1923), which he named after the most modern express locomotive. A composition inspired by sport was called *Rugby*.

The most ordinary things in everyday life can become the subject for a musical composition. Darius Milhaud, also one of the

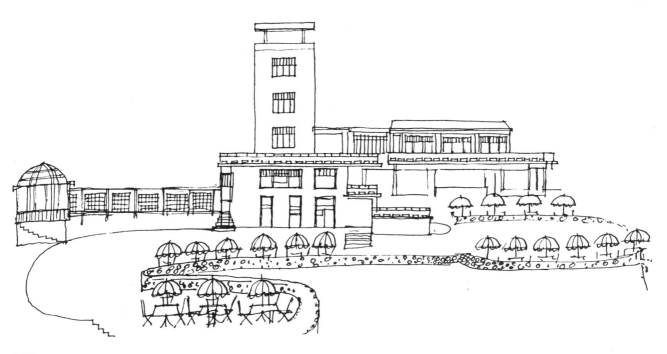

'Six', set *A Catalogue of Flowers* and *A Catalogue of Agricultural Machinery* to music. An Austrian composer, Ernst Křenek, set a train timetable to music. Paul Hindemith depicted the year 1922 in a jazz piano suite and Bohuslav Martinů, the Czech composer then living in Paris, wrote a symphonic movement, *Half-Time,* creating an image of the excited mood at a stadium during half-time at a football match. In admiration of the courageous flight of Charles Lindberg, *La Bagarre* ('The Tumult'), stimulated by the sight of the chaotic crowds in the streets of Paris, was dedicated to him. The same event was the theme of a composition by the German composer **Kurt Weill** (1900–50), *Lindberg Flug.*

Musical expression was simplified. In reaction to the romantic mood, a more ordinary expression and classical restraint were sought. A new musical trend was created, Neo-Classicism.

Technical progress has never ceased. It is always bringing new surprises, although perhaps today we do not experience them with the thrill that our ancestors did. While they were exultant over the express locomotive, we take interplanetary flight for granted. If the arts reflect our present civilization in a new way, these reflections could, in the future, become an image of the past. If they survive their own day, it will not be so much for their subject matter as for their masterly artistic shaping.

There is one source of inspi-

Right: **Sunlit countryside, always an inspiration for the artists.**

If you can read music, you will recognize that this excerpt from Camille Saint-Saëns' *Carnival of the Animals* is the clucking of hens and the crowing of cockerels.

ration that has remainded unchanged from epoch to epoch and this will be our last stopping place on our journey through the world of music.

The Song of Nature

It is impossible to resist the sounds that fill nature. When we are most in a hurry, we still stand a while to listen to the song of the blackbird, the call of the cuckoo or the croaking of frogs in a pond. We are disturbed by the barking of a neighbour's dog, we are numb with anxiety at the rumbling of thunder and we are calmed by the whisper in the tops of trees or the murmuring mountain stream.

Tanagra, a song bird from the American countryside. The first excerpt is the approximative transcription of its song, the second excerpt is from Antonín Dvořák's *String Quartet in F major*.

The flute can imitate the song of birds perfectly, as Olivier Messiaen showed, for example, in his composition *The Blackbird*.

It is not surprising that impressions from nature have found an echo in works of art, whether through using music to describe similar feelings or through direct copying of the voices of nature.

Beethoven entitled the first movement in his *Pastoral Symphony* 'Awakening of joyful feelings on arrival in the country'. With his overture to *Der Freischütz*, von Weber issues an invitation to enjoy the romantic scenery of the forest. In his symphonic poem *From the Czech Meadows and Woods*, Smetana opens up a wide, sunlit countryside for the listener.

No one could ever count the number of times the cuckoo, the nightingale and the blackbird have sounded in instrumental pieces, or how many times a composer has imitated the thunder of horses' hooves or the buzzing of insects.

A classic example of a work about nature is the *Carnival of the Animals* by Camille Saint-Saëns, in which one can hear hens and cockerels, donkeys, lions, the cuckoo and even the swan singing its sad song. Antelopes race in a wild gallop, the tortoise deliberately shuffles forward to a version of Offenbach's cancan, slowed down many times, and the elephant dances its ponderous waltz. However, do not just look for an imitation of the sounds of nature or a picture of its inhabitants in this music. For the composer, this is just an excuse for the unleashing of his very uncommon musical humour. How, otherwise, could two *pianists* have found their way into this company of animals? Evidently, it was because Saint-Saëns was annoyed by the eternal repetition of finger exercises.

Antonín Dvořák was a great lover of the outdoors. When he spent a holiday in the American village of Spillville, Iowa, he heard the song of an unfamiliar bird. He remembered this song when he composed the scherzo movement of his *String Quartet in F major*.

Leoš Janáček recorded fragments of human speech in musical notation and used them in his vocal works. He also knew intimately all sorts of sounds from the forests and town parks. In his *Cunning Little Vixen*, the forest sings with the harmonies of its many voices.

The French composer **Olivier**

The Cunning Little Vixen by **Leoš Janáček is an opera about nature and people, about the eternal wheel of life. In the upper picture we see the fox, Golden Mane courting the Little Vixen. Beneath it is the closing scene of the opera.**

Music has always been a gratifying theme for the visual arts. This painting, called *The Accordion Player*, was completed in 1913 by the Czech artist Josef Čapek (1887–1945).

Messiaen (1908–92) was intrigued by the songs of birds and used them in a number of works, for example in his piano concerto *Le Reveil des Oiseaux* ('The Awakening of the Birds'), in his *Exotic Birds* for the piano and orchestra and in his piece for the piano *Catalogue of Birds*.

A work of art is not a documentary photograph. The artist portrays the countryside on his canvas in a way that is often quite different from how it actually looks. He sees it in his own way, and from his visual information creates a picture according to his own artistic concept. Even less can a composer copy sound reality. If truly natural sounds appear in his work, then they are, as a rule, just the means for developing a broader idea.

The essence of musical creation lies elsewhere. Music has formed its own world of sound in which it uses its own means of expression. It is bound to the rest of the world with a thousand ties; nature is only one of them.

Epilogue

It must be said that, in the pages of this book, the most important thing is missing — music. It is as if we were to write about painting without seeing a single picture or to discuss poetry without reading a single verse. Pictures of instruments, musicians, the countryside and buildings can, at most, call to mind the music we have at some time heard.

So let this last paragraph be an invitation to the real world of music, to the world of resounding music that unfolds outside the pages of every book. It is there that you can experience the unforgettable adventure of music.

Name Index

Page numbers in *italic* refer to illustrations.